DESIGN MOM

DESIGN MOM

HOW TO LIVE WITH KIDS: A ROOM-BY-ROOM GUIDE

GABRIELLE STANLEY BLAIR

ARTISAN

NEW YORK

Library of Congress Cataloging-in-Publication Data

Blair, Gabrielle Stanley.
  Design mom : how to live with kids : a room-by-room guide
/ Gabrielle Stanley Blair.
     pages cm
  ISBN 978-1-57965-571-6
  1. Interior decoration—Human factors. 2. Families.
  3. Interior decoration. I. Title.
  NK2115.B53 2015
  747'.1—dc23   2014038734

Design by Naomi Mizusaki, Supermarket

Artisan books are available at special discounts when
purchased in bulk for premiums and sales promotions as well
as for fund-raising or educational use. Special editions or
book excerpts also can be created to specification. For details,
contact the Special Sales Director at the address below, or
send an e-mail to specialmarkets@workman.com.

Published by Artisan
A division of Workman Publishing Company, Inc.
225 Varick Street
New York, NY 10014-4381
artisanbooks.com

Published simultaneously in Canada
by Thomas Allen & Son, Limited

Printed in Canada
First printing, March 2015

10 9 8 7 6 5 4 3 2 1

To Mike and Donna, my own Design Parents.

Thank you, Dad, for introducing teenage me to Macintosh computers and "desktop publishing." Thank you, Mom, for allowing me to make design decisions at an early age, and for showing me that it doesn't take deep pockets to create a beautiful place where your family can thrive.

CONTENTS

INTRODUCTION

IF you asked me to describe myself in a few words, I'd tell you that I'm a designer and a mother of six. If you gave me a few more, I might tell you that I've been a blogger called Design Mom since my fifth child was born—almost nine years ago!—writing daily about all those areas where motherhood and design intersect. There's also Alt Summit, a business conference I cofounded for pioneering and rookie bloggers and creatives of all kinds, as well as Olive Us, a video series created by my husband, Ben Blair, and me, that features our kids—Ralph, Maude, Olive, Oscar, Betty, and Flora June—having adventures and learning new things and being good to each other. But my favorite words to use to describe myself are the ones I wrote first.

I *love* the topic of this book: how to live with kids. And not just how to live, but how to live *well*. How to create a home that appeals to you as a grown-up, and suits your kids at all their ages and stages. This topic is on my mind daily—no exaggeration. I think about the kids' bathroom, and how if I would simply stock the drawer with a couple of extra hairbrushes, wails of "I can't find the hairbrush and I'm going to be late!" during the morning rush might be avoided. It's a little thing, but it could prevent the day from going downhill

first thing in the morning. I remember the art in my childhood home (oh, the prints in that oversize Norman Rockwell book!), and then consider the art in my current home and wonder what sort of impact it's having on my kids and if I should change it up to create a new or different sort of impact.

Since our first son, Ralph, was born seventeen years ago, one of the biggest things I've learned is that design doesn't have to disappear when kids appear. You can definitely, absolutely have a beautiful home that works for both kids and adults (and babies too!). It's totally possible to take the space you live in right now and figure out how it can best serve your family's needs. I'm 100 percent confident that you can create a place where every member of the family feels right at home.

To my mind, a thoughtfully designed home is one of the greatest gifts you can give to your family. The items you've chosen to surround you, both the practical and the decorative, tell your family's story. They foster important conversations. They influence the likes and dislikes of your family members. They have the ability to prevent or cause frustration. They form the backdrop to your child's childhood.

I also know that the practice of living a well-designed life with kids—one or six or however many happen to be running through your house—

is a continual effort. The system that works for your family today might not work tomorrow, when the piano-lesson schedule changes, or when summer vacation starts. I find that incredibly comforting. It means there is no due date for my house (or your house) to be "done." There is no to-do list of tasks I have to accomplish right away to make sure my home is wonderful. I can implement one idea today, solve a recurring problem tomorrow, and over time create an inviting haven that makes for the best sort of family memories.

Design isn't some froufrou gloss or shiny veneer on life, it's insisting on a solution (preferably an elegant one) and working carefully to make sure that solution works within whatever constraints you have—architectural, financial, or the fact that children live in your home. I know for a fact that you can use design to solve problems in your home. I've had a million (well, technically, a lot less than a million) conversations with readers and other parents about how to make their nitty-gritty, day-to-day duties more intentional, more stylish, and, dare I suggest, way easier. And every week on DesignMom.com I feature a peek into a home somewhere in the world to showcase how others are living well-designed lives with their children. Every week, I'm shocked at the fresh inspiration. It never ends!

So if you asked me to describe this book in just a few words, I'd tell you that I'm a designer and a mother of six and that my husband and I love to imagine and work hard at designing our home environment, that this is how we strive to live well together. If you gave me a few more, I might tell you that I wrote this book to inspire you and give you some stylish, simple solutions for your own home. But the truest description of this book is the one I wrote first. I'm a mom and I'm a designer, and some of my best family memories are made when those roles collide. I'm so glad to be able to share with you the secrets I've learned along the way.

P.S. If you glanced at the contents, you may have noticed that there's no chapter on the master bedroom. That's intentional. You don't need my advice here. The master bedroom is not a kid zone, it's *your* zone, and you can make it as fabulous as you please. But it wouldn't hurt to keep a favorite storybook or two in your nightstand, and perhaps an extra blanket and a floor pad under the bed for middle-of-the-night visitors who had a bad dream.

THE ENTRYWAY

If you've got a foyer and a mudroom, you're one lucky bird. We've lived in eight different houses since we married, and six of those had front doors that opened directly onto the living room. But something I've discovered over the years of growing our family is that no matter the layout of the house, setting up a functional entry is key to gracefully managing a home with kids.

Our current home doesn't have a mudroom or a closet in the foyer. But with a little creative thinking, a well-thought-out piece of furniture, clean colors, and smart hooks, we were able to turn a long, narrow hallway just off the entry into a space that works as hard as one twice its size. Bonus points that it keeps all those mudroom items neatly out of sight of arriving guests, while still making them easily accessible for running-out-the-door schoolkids.

Is it possible to create a functional entryway and still make a winning first impression in what is probably the smallest space in your entire home? I say yes. Your home begins and ends with the entry. Go ahead and make it great.

01

ASSESS THE SITUATION

Think back to the first wintry day you walked through the door of your current home. You probably removed your parka and scarf right away, then slipped off your boots. Was there a convenient place to hoard your heap? If you have a front closet, naturally, that might make the most sense. But what if your things are wet, and the thought of storing them in a tiny enclosed area gives you mildew-y shivers?

It's the same situation no matter the weather; every season comes with its own stuff. Consider how many people will be removing their outerwear, dumping their beach towels, kicking off boots, and closing their umbrellas, as well as the reality of the space available—then make your plan. You may conclude that you need two closet hangers for every person, or a stack of washable rugs at the ready. You may decide to go for sturdy wall hooks hung over a bench, or a row of old-school gym lockers. Whatever you choose, make sure it works for all the people who will be using it, family and guests, adults and toddlers alike.

We don't have a closet in our current entryway, so we chose Bjärnum folding wall hooks from Ikea to corral all our seasonal accessories. They can be pulled down when you need them but folded up when you don't! When they're open, the hooks are deep enough to hold multiple items—we use them for jackets and hats, gym bags, and our reusable shopping totes. We installed them at three different heights, with two hooks especially for June that she can easily reach, encouraging her four-year-old independence and introducing her to the concept of responsibility.

Opposite: Don't have room for hooks or storage in your entry? Consider annexing a nearby space. We turned this standard 48-inch-wide hallway into a "mudroom" with wall hooks, cubbies for backpacks, a paperwork station, and a stool. It's just around the corner from the front door and keeps the coming-and-going chaos out of sight.

02

AIM FOR FUNCTION + BEAUTY

Think of the beautiful teapot you use every single day. It does its job well and seems to get prettier with age. It makes you happy when you see it each morning. This should be your goal when choosing any object in your home—high function + high beauty.

The thing you want to avoid is low function + low beauty. It's the garbage can that came with the house. You disliked its odd proportions on sight, and then the dislike turned to hate when you realized the lid didn't work. But life gets busy and somehow you haven't replaced it, even though it bugs you every time you have to interact with it. (Don't waste another second hating that thing. Replace that darn trash can ASAP.)

Sometimes, things in the low beauty + high function or low function + high beauty quadrants are objects you simply "make do" with—but other times, those items are treasures. When we're talking about low beauty + high function, it might be something like that ugly showerhead that has the perfect water pressure. When you redid your bathroom, you tried a sleek new version, but it could barely wash out your shampoo, so you reinstalled the old, reliable one. Maybe someday, you'll find a gorgeous showerhead with perfect water pressure. But if not, this sturdy, not-fancy option will keep you company.

An example of low function + high beauty is the rocking chair you inherited from your great-aunt. If you're honest with yourself, it's not comfortable at all, but oh! It's so beautiful, and it reminds you of your favorite aunt every time you see it. I say, feel free to keep around anything that makes you smile when it catches your eye.

Opposite: A tight hallway transforms into a hardworking entry that has it all: a place to put on shoes, a narrow table for holding keys and signing permission slips, and simple hooks for hats and coats.

03

SHOE STORAGE IS YOUR BEST FRIEND

The number of shoes in your house may be comical at this point—flip-flops, rain boots, sneakers, ballet shoes, soccer cleats, patent-leather Sunday-best Mary Janes. That's why having a place for everything is critical, because scattered shoes are the best way to turn an entryway into an obstacle course. Happily, you have storage options—from shoe racks in the front closet to shoe shelves under a bench. But before you make a purchase or search out a DIY project to solve your shoe situation, decide which shoes are going to live where.

Determine what can stay in the bedroom and what has to be easily accessible in the entry, then figure out storage to match your needs. I only store in the entryway shoes that we tend to grab on the way out the door. In the Oakland summer, it's flip-flops or sandals. They don't take up much space, so a small metal bin is all we need to hold them. For our Colorado winters, snow boots were lined up neatly on the floor, but Sunday shoes were kept in the bedroom closets.

Opposite, clockwise from top left: Every family handles shoe storage a bit differently. Whether you employ gym-worthy lockers, place a simple basket under an entry bench, repurpose found wooden cubbies, or just line shoes up in a row, let these photos inspire you to find a solution that works for your house.

04

LET YOUR COATS AND SHOES COME OUT OF THE CLOSET

As William Morris wisely advised, "Have nothing in your house that you do not know to be useful, or believe to be beautiful." Ideally, items in your home are both useful *and* beautiful. They can serve a utilitarian purpose and can also be displayed.

Your fabulous new trench coat definitely qualifies! Simply hang your favorite togs à la Macy's holiday window display for a functional, beautiful storage solution. In rainy Normandy, our row of wellies—in heights and colors that reflected all eight family members—was one of the most charming parts of our decor.

Above: A customized coatrack takes advantage of unused nooks and crannies. The built-in bench has storage beneath.
Opposite: Keeping your heaviest, thickest coats on display means less crowded, more usable closets.

AT THE BLAIR HOUSE

BENDING THE RULES

Every well-run home has rules: respect each other's space and belongings, zero swearing (unless you step on a Lego), don't flush toys down the toilet, water balloons and Popsicles outside only, and no shoes inside the house. That last rule can be tricky, especially with guests who aren't used to it, aren't wearing cute socks, or are a little embarrassed by their chipped pedicures. And if you find yourself living in an indoor/outdoor kind of home (raising my hand here) where the kids are five minutes in, five minutes out, five minutes in on repeat all day long, the shoes-off rule simply doesn't work.

So depending on your visitors or the realities of your home, be prepared to budge at a moment's notice. In fact, this is almost a mantra for living with kids: Make rules and guidelines for the best vision of your home that you can, but always be willing to adjust to the current situation. Some rules are meant to be broken.

05

USE YOUR WALLS

Every child defaults to dropping stuff on the floor as she enters the house, but if the floor is crowded, the whole house feels chaotic. So guard your floor space whenever you can and find a better option for that pile of school things. Something easily accessible for fetching homework assignments when the after-school snacks are eaten, and near the entry so that everything is ready to go on mornings when everyone seems to be running behind.

Vertical solutions keep your floor zone clear, so that everything has its place without being underfoot. Lightweight preschool backpacks, for example, are perfect candidates to hang on wall hooks.

Since my family can practically fill a classroom, I've found that using school storage as a model has worked well for us. In one house, we used a set of vintage blue lockers—they were big enough to fit multiple jackets and parkas and sturdy enough for heavy, book-laden backpacks. School-inspired cubbies (think shelves with cubed compartments) have also done the trick.

Opposite: School notes will never get lost again, thanks to this clever clipboards-on-hooks system. And the wall-mounted pencil sharpener eliminates one more excuse when the kids are avoiding getting their homework done.

06

GEAR UP WITH BASKETS, BUCKETS, AND MORE

Kids come with all sorts of gear—and it multiplies! Seemingly overnight, one hat and a pair of gloves turns into five hats, two scarves, and seven mittens. In the summer, this happens with beach towels, goggles, and water toys. And those kid-size odds and ends need to live somewhere.

We've used crates at the bottom of a front closet. We've used a good-looking basket just inside the front door. In our current setup, a shelf full of cubbies stores beach towels in the summer and backpacks throughout the school year.

Instead of an umbrella stand, we favor a hardworking, handsome bucket. It's a cute and useful addition to any foyer because it can hold a number of items needed quickly upon flight from the house. These include lacrosse sticks, ninja swords, a favorite walking branch, and even an umbrella or two!

I feel I should note here that I don't think there is a perfect storage solution for all the moving parts in a family's life. I've tried hooks, clothespin lines, and plastic storage boxes for each kid. Even with the strictest vigilance, seasonal accoutrements go rogue two weeks into the season. But when you're faced with a lone glove, it's nice to know just where to put it while it waits for its mate to someday reappear.

Opposite: This mix of casual striped baskets with luxe tabletop accessories makes a pretty statement that represents the realities of a family.

07

A PLACE TO SIT, IF ONLY FOR A MINUTE OR TWO

The seating inside the front door will welcome you home on even the craziest days. Use it to set down your bags or frowning toddler, or collapse there yourself. The only way it could get any better is if someone magically appeared to offer you a massage!

No matter how tiny your space may be, there should be a place to sit in your foyer. It's a place to wait for the school bus while double-knotting laces, continue a neighborly conversation, or add a last-minute hair clip to your four-year-old's curls.

Above: These lightweight entry perches can be split apart if needed and moved to another room to provide extra chairs for guests or double as low side tables.

SMALL-SPACE SEATING

1

BENCHES

Benches are miracle workers. They offer seating and storage and pretend to be a table in a pinch. Stacked, they even work as bookshelves. They come in all sizes and have unlimited potential to work in every room of the house. I love a rugged, weathered bench in the entry, something that looks right at home with muddy boots beneath. But I also like sleek, modern benches and those with shelf space below for wire bins that hold mittens and hats. When the kids set up a concert hall in the living room, or there are extra guests for dinner, the bench in your front hall will come to the rescue.

2

POUFS, CHAKKIS, AND OTHER EXOTIC TOUCHES

Small spaces are ideal for experimentation. Maybe your heart beats faster when you touch fragile Japanese silks or run your hand over Spanish tiles or Balinese carvings. Instead of overwhelming your entire home with themes from faraway lands, add just a touch of what interests you the most. Foyers are the simplest spots to fill your adventurous design cravings. Rather than buy ten daring chairs to surround a dining table, you can choose one for the entry and see what it's like without making a big commitment. Or try some well-traveled seating, like leather Moroccan poufs, chakkis with colorful cushions, or a lean tufted bench covered in fabric—like batik or a suzani.

3

DOUBLE-DUTY FURNISHINGS

If space is at a premium, choose furnishings that aren't afraid to work overtime. A trunk makes a great seat, and it also stores an extra quilt or your Halloween decorations. Look for ottomans that open, or painted chests, and consider a low-height ladder or step stool that can work as a chair when it's not being used for its intended purpose.

08

MAKE YOUR SHOES-OFF POLICY EASIER FOR YOUR GUESTS

What's your footwear philosophy for those who enter your home? If you're a shoes-off family and it's a rule you plan to stick with, you should make it easy and inviting to follow. Make sure there's a comfortable place to sit, and shoe storage within easy reach. And I highly recommend hanging an extra-long-handled shoehorn in plain view of where your guests remove and replace their shoes. It makes the whole process less of an awkward, bent-over, falling-against-the-wall endeavor, and more of a civilized ritual!

Above: Consider providing a basket of fresh anklets for visitors who don't love the idea of walking around barefoot.

09

ROLL OUT THE RED CARPET

The foyer rug is integral to your happiness. I'm dead serious. As Erma Bombeck wisely wrote, "All of us have moments in our lives that test our courage. Taking children into a house with a white carpet is one of them." For the next few years, while you've got dirty little boots and muddy Chucks traipsing through your house, invest in an easy-to-clean foyer rug that will work hard for your family.

Your foyer rug needs to absorb drips from rain boots, and the noise of pattering feet. It needs to withstand a hundred entries and exits a day. And since it will be one of the first things you see when you enter the house, and the last thing you see as you leave, it might as well be gorgeous. (Turn the page for a few of my favorite options.)

Left: Mix it up! Here, an easy-to-clean, practical runner handles muddy feet at the entrance, while a color-rich woven beauty draws guests (and residents) into the home.

RUGS THAT WORK FOR FAMILIES

1 WOOL

If you're seeking natural, environmentally friendly fibers in your foyer, wool carpets are probably the most enduring and the warmest. We've used them for practically every room in our home at some point. They hide soil wonderfully when woven in dark colors or complex patterns, and they respond favorably to cleaning—so you shouldn't cringe too much when dusty feet walk through your front door. Wool is naturally flame-retardant and even repels moisture. The only downside is that wool rugs sometimes shed like mad, filling up my vacuum every time I do a quick cleaning.

2 COTTON

Cotton is soft to the touch and wears just like your favorite T-shirt from college. I've never tried a cotton floor covering on a large scale. Instead, I opt for inexpensive cotton rugs that are small enough to throw in the washing machine. When we're caught off guard by a rainstorm, a stack of cotton rag rugs to receive wet footsteps saves the day. One caveat: If you're living in a colder climate, you may want to pass, because cotton won't be your warmest option.

3 JUTE

Add texture to any room with jute, an eco-friendly material constructed from natural fibers and often hand-woven with a mix of other plant strands. We currently have a thick braided jute rug in our boys' bedroom, and we love it for its durability, its ease at blending seamlessly into virtually any decor, and its capacity to hide most dirt stains.

4 SISAL

Sisal, a stiff natural fiber, is a marvelous investment for areas that don't include the threat of wetness. It's sophisticated, long-lasting, colorfast, and static-free—but it is expensive. I've seen it used beautifully in family homes, but if you're starting out, having babies, or moving from state to state, I think jute is the way to go.

5 WOVEN VINYL

Woven vinyl is another fiber favorite in family homes, both for its durability in high-traffic areas (indoor and out!) and its easy-to-clean factor. Yes, some options look plastic-y and tacky, but these days you can also find generous woven options that have a nautical rope feel, and range from earth-tone goodness to modern bold statements. My sister uses thick versions as runners in her high-traffic hallway and they hold up beautifully. They're mold- and mildew-resistant and light enough for a quick shakeout on the front porch, and they can be scrubbed outside with a hose and dish soap when they need a thorough cleaning.

6 PERSIANS

I know, I know . . . the cost! But there's a reason Persians lay around for a hundred years and still garner insane prices: They last and last and last. They are visually remarkable and instantly add a historical and luxe flavor to any room. Choose darker shades or varied patterns to hide your family's dirt, and try to nab one with a high knot density that can withstand cat claws, dogs digging for imaginary bones, and most childhoods! But be warned: The higher the knot density, the more expensive the rug. (If you like the exotic feel of eastern decor but a Persian isn't in your budget, Turkish kilims are made to endure and are much cheaper than a true Oriental rug.)

10

CREATE A COMMAND CENTER

Near the entry there should be a table or shelf or cabinet where you can keep a collection of essentials like pens and note cards, an extra cell-phone charger or two, and a little bowl to hold spare change.

In some houses, we have also included a small chalkboard or whiteboard to write notes for those coming and going—"Don't forget, piano lesson at five o'clock!" or "Do you need anything at the grocery?" or "Have an awesome day. I love you guys!"—but since the cell-phone invasion, I send most of these sweet little notes as texts.

This is also a good spot to leave your car keys, findable by anyone in the house who might have left a backpack or a trombone in the car. This mini command center should be accessible to the whole family.

Opposite: Trays are lifesavers. I use them to corral assorted objects in many rooms in the house, but they're especially useful in an entryway.

11

YOUR FIRST LINE OF DEFENSE AGAINST PAPERWORK

The amount of paperwork that comes into a family home every single day is astounding, and it can pile up so fast it feels like some sort of spell is involved. Having a place to sort and store mail and other papers until you have a moment to deal with them is a huge advantage when trying to keep organized.

That's why one of the first things I include in our entry is a letter box or file sorter. In our current house, entry space is tight, so our paper organizer is the vertical sort, attached to the wall. It holds permission slips and other signed forms, teacher notes, party invitations, thank-you cards ready to be mailed, and the one or two bills that we don't pay online—really, everything that comes in the mailbox or is left on the front porch, plus the things we shouldn't forget when we're about to leave for the day.

Establishing a designated paper space doesn't mean things won't fall through the cracks. But it does mean that when your third grader calls from school in a panic because she forgot her field trip permission slip, you'll know just where to find it.

Above: A multitiered organizer can be used in many ways: a slot for each family member, or for designating different kinds of paperwork and tasks.

12

THROW IT OUT BEFORE IT COMES IN

We keep a cute recycling tin, otherwise known as the circular file, within close reach of our entry paper center. Junk mail and unwanted catalogs are gleefully dropped in, as well as any paper flyers we don't really need. Instant filing, no categorization or alphabetization necessary!

Next to the recycling bin, I recommend a small trash can, too, to collect the random candy wrappers and dried-out markers that inevitably emerge from backpacks.

Right: This little trash can's lid has a hook so that you can rest it on the side of the bin. (I love Ikea!)

CHIC CEMENT PLANTERS
WARM UP YOUR FRONT PORCH FOR UNDER $10

I love the modern, industrial look of cement planters, but I find them cost prohibitive—especially in large sizes, and especially if I want to group several to greet guests at our front door. So I figured out a simple way to make some at home. The main ingredients are cinder blocks and a cement mix made for resurfacing. This project is so inexpensive and easy, you'll want to make a dozen!

MATERIALS

Landscape cement glue and four 12-inch concrete pavers (for large planter) or single cinder block (for small planter)

Ardex Feather Finish cement mix in gray

Small hand trowel

Hand sander or sandpaper block

Rag or sponge

Concrete sealant

STEP 1: For the large planter, create a cube using cement glue and the four pavers, with an open bottom and top. For the small planter, any small concrete cinder block will work. No gluing necessary.

STEP 2: Mix the Ardex Feather Finish with water, two parts cement mix to one part water. If needed, add water until the consistency is similar to that of thick pancake batter. Use a small hand trowel to spread the cement in a thin layer (approximately ⅛ inch thick) on all four sides and the top surface of the concrete cube. It does not need to be "neat" or perfectly smooth.

STEP 3: Once the cement is dry (this can take several hours, or even overnight depending on the weather), use a hand sander or sanding block to sand down any obtrusive cement ridges so that the surface feels generally smooth. Again, it should not be perfect. The goal is to have the marks from the trowel, and any inconsistencies in the cement, show up on the surface.

STEP 4: Using a household rag or sponge, apply concrete sealant to the sanded surface. Let it dry, and your cement planter is ready to hold potted plants. If you'd like to plant directly in the planter, use a piece of burlap or mesh to create a "cup" or "bowl" at the bottom of the cube to hold the soil, while still allowing water to pass through.

13

ARTWORK: HOW YOUR ENTRY SAYS HELLO

A piece of art in your entry will act as eye contact, a firm handshake, and a heartfelt "Pleased to meet you" to everyone who rings your bell, introducing you in the best way possible. When you display art that's important to all of you, you're telling guests more about yourselves than most conversations ever could. Choose something that lends joy to your home's shiny first impression.

More important, choose something that you won't mind having seared into your children's memories for life. Because the artwork in the entryway will be the last thing they see as they head out into the world on their first day of kindergarten, and the first thing they see when they come home after a tough day in middle school. It's one more opportunity to shape your kids into the upstanding, high-functioning, lovely adults you want them to be.

Above: In this entry, bold wall art makes for a memorable statement and a conversation starter, while the tabletop hosts an ever-changing collection of tactile sculptures, ceramics, and assorted objects that are both beautiful and practical.

ART THAT SETS THE TONE: 4 ENTRY-WORTHY IDEAS

1. VINTAGE SIGNAGE: You can't go wrong with a classic welcome sign. You could also seek out an old metal office sign rummaged from a flea market: RETURN LOST ITEMS HERE. Or find a new sign, made to look old, with a little more cheek: UNATTENDED CHILDREN WILL BE GIVEN FREE PUPPIES. If you'd like to display the family initial, salvage an oversize version from a gas-station sign.

2. LYRICS, SLOGANS, AND ENCOURAGING WORDS: "You Are My Sunshine." "It's Going to Be a Great Day!" "Work Hard, Play Hard." Search for popular sayings or lyrics on Etsy to find prints and posters. Or hire a graphic designer to make a poster just for you.

3. A JOLT OF POSITIVITY: Colorful pieces featuring flowers and sunshine and happiness influence the feeling in your home. Think fresh yellows and greens, or sunny reds and pinks.

4. TRAVEL PHOTOS OR POSTERS: Since family members leave and return from this point, travel-themed art works wonderfully here. Maybe something you shot yourself on an epic family trip! Or a classic travel poster featuring a destination on your family's wish list. You could even celebrate where you live right this minute—hang a photograph of the view from a picturesque hike, a street shot that shows a bit of your beloved doughnut shop, or a photograph of a memorable mural.

14

KEEP YOUR FAMILY RUNNING ON TIME

Keeping appointments matters. Being on time for them matters, too. Though much of our time-watching happens on phones or tablets, I like to have a wall clock where the whole family can see it. I don't particularly enjoy rushing my family out the door, but there are occasions when it's important to pay attention to time. Before I send my kids outside to play, we glance at the clock by the door, decide when they should return, and make sure everyone is on the same page. A well-placed timepiece will also keep you company during those nights spent pacing prior to curfew.

A clock is an easy way to express some family style. Do you prefer oversize, digital, maybe retro? For years, we've hung a clock that looks like it was swiped from a high school gymnasium. In the entry of the home I grew up in, there was an antique wall clock that my parents had inherited. We would wind it with a key, and my mother kept a little toy mouse in the bottom—"Hickory Dickory Dock."

One year, when we were living all over the world, my siblings and I gave our parents five identical clocks and on each one we added a plaque listing a different city: New York, Frankfurt, Bogotá, Athens, Salt Lake City. Each clock was set to the corresponding time zone. For those of you with far-flung family and friends, it's a sweet notion that you may be beginning a day while a loved one is ending their own.

Opposite: To mimic this faux wallpaper, gather maps of all sorts—relics from *National Geographic*, star charts, subway maps—then tack them to the wall with pins, double-sided tape, or wall putty. Layer and overlap them until the wall is covered.

15

LET THERE BE LIGHT (and dimmers)

Like everything you bring into your house, the lighting you choose for your entry can say whatever you want it to say. Perhaps the fixtures you're drawn to are a seamless part of the architecture and do their work without drawing attention, like a really good concierge, ready to welcome you and make your day as easy as possible. Or you could go for lighting that contrasts with the architectural style of your home, its vibrant lampshade surprising you a bit every time you catch sight of it. In this scenario it is like the fun aunt of the house: the one who gives your kids candy, hires a pony for their birthday parties, and makes even a random Tuesday feel special. That's the beauty of a foyer—it's a small space, so feel free to play around with it.

Above: The simplest entryways make for the calmest comings and goings. Instead of using a traditional console table or exposed cubbies, add feet to a basic cabinet, then hide the backpacks and paperwork and general chaos inside.

LIGHT AS A TOOL: 4 WAYS TO BRIGHTEN YOUR ENTRYWAY

1. TASK LIGHT: You'll be so glad if you have a task light near your entryway "command center" (see page 35). On gray, sluggish mornings, it will assist you as you fill out forms for the gymnastics team sign-ups and put your signature on report cards. It will illuminate the estimate the landscaping team dropped by, and help you pen a thank-you note.

2. FLASHLIGHT: A ready flashlight is more of a need than a want. It's essential if the power goes out on a stormy night. And when your baby can't seem to fall asleep, and you're exhausted from pacing the hallway, it will help to shed light under the lockers to hunt down that lost pacifier.

3. TABLE AND FLOOR LAMPS: A floor lamp with a dimmer, or a table lamp on a foyer console table, will offer bright light to welcome the family home at the end of the day, and lower light to ease evening into bedtime. Table and floor lamps come in so many styles, they're a great way to add interest and a new decor element to the space.

4. LIGHT SWITCH: In new construction, this might be a no-brainer, but in older homes it's not common at all. A light switch just inside the front door is a relief when the whole family stumbles in from a road trip late at night. Choose one with a tiny nightlight built in and you won't have to grope around to find it.

THE LIVING ROOM

What's in my living room? Simply put, everything I want my kids to ask about and discuss and talk about some more. I want the items in this room to fill them with ideas and encourage them to ask a million questions. The answers might be found among the stacks of books, or they might be found after a long conversation. Either way is pretty wonderful.

I think of the living room as the candy shop of our home. It's a sweet reward after a hectic morning or a never-ending day. There are meaningful images on the walls, items reflecting current events and pop culture on the coffee table, and family collections at kid eye level.

I'm not entirely sure there's one perfect formula for a living room designed for life, but I know what works for us. No matter where we've lived or our home's square footage, we make sure our living room can hold a conversation from which we have to drag ourselves away. When the conversation starts to fade, a quick glance around the room sparks it once again. And when that fails, we pull out the guitars!

01

DESIGN YOUR LIVING ROOM TO BE USED DAILY

Despite its friendly name, the living room has historically been off-limits to the under-five set. Many families reserve the space for special occasions, special guests, or simply those who know how to live without making a mess, patting down little ones before allowing entrance: no markers, no scissors, no brownies, and don't even think about muddy shoes!

I don't believe in unused rooms or unused things in any family home, no matter its size. To me, reserving a space for people who may pop in a few times a year is a missed opportunity for memory-making.

Make it easy for your family to truly live in your living room. Whatever your preferred activities, there are a million ways to ensure that the room is used the way you've designed it. If you want the living room to function as a reading nook, make sure there's enough lighting to brighten your pages. If it's your family's cozy space, make sure there are plenty of throws and a music docking system within reach. Form follows function: Once you've determined how the room will be used, you can make it gorgeous, choosing materials, furniture, and accents that work best for the plan you've made.

Opposite: This pink Moroccan pouf can be used as extra seating, a footstool, or a play table for a toddler. The rocking horse is ready to entertain, without taking up lots of visual attention.

02

DON'T RUSH

In our California home, it took about seven months to figure out how our living room would best work for us. We took our time, observing how the kids interacted with the room, and making adjustments from there. When I could see we weren't taking enough advantage of the wall of windows, a major (and fantastic) feature of the room, I added a long row of benches to help us enjoy the view and provide additional seating. Instead of a traditional sofa and loveseat combo, I figured out that two smallish sofas made better use of the not-so-big space. And because the house is surrounded by trees and is shady most of the day, I kept everything in a light, neutral palette—floors, walls, furniture, artwork—to reflect the light and keep the room from feeling gloomy.

Allow your living room to inform you how it's going to be used; it will tell you, but you have to listen! This process may take many months full of family jam sessions, political discussions, the nightly reading aloud of Harry Potter books, and one birthday piñata in the shape of a hot-air balloon, but taking the time to think carefully about how the room is currently being used, and how it needs to be used, will result in a thoughtful, beautiful, workable living space.

Opposite: This sofa's interesting profile was one of the main reasons I chose it for our living room—it's one of the first things you see when you enter our house.

03

START WITH SEATING

The first step in designing your living room is ensuring that there are enough places and spaces to allow for a comfortable conversation between all the members of your family, at least. There are eight Blairs in my house, which means that if I didn't have seating for eight in my living room, it would officially be crowned our most poorly designed room! That is not an honor I want any room to win.

For our living rooms past and present, I've resisted the oversize sectional whenever possible. Sure, sectionals seem like they offer the most seating capacity and comfort—but they also limit your room's configuration. If ever you get the itch to rearrange or switch up your furniture room to room, a large piece makes that more of an impossibility. And forget clearing the area to make room for a recital or other special family event that requires floor space; that sectional isn't going anywhere! My family simply needs more flexibility than an oversize sofa can provide.

I've found that using a mix of chairs, love seats, poufs, and perhaps even a sturdy ottoman on which to perch, is a more stylish, more versatile, and more vibrant decor strategy. With a variety of smaller pieces to arrange as we need them, we're ready for almost anything that happens in that room, formally or informally. And the poufs and ottomans perform double duty, either as extra guest seating or, topped with a tray, pretending to be a coffee table.

Opposite: One of the things I love about this room is that no two seating options are the same. There's a bench in the background, a red classic formal upholstered chair, a modern chair with a sheepskin throw, a woven pouf, a comfy couch—even a swing!

04

COUCH MATTERS (because the couch matters so, so much)

To me, a living room couch should be one of the most intentional purchases in your home, on par with your kitchen appliances and the bed in which you dream nightly. A couch can say just as much about your personality and your life as . . . well . . . your personality and your life!

Before choosing a couch, draft a few questions for every potential contender—like a job interview, but without the jitters! Couches are meant to be a long-term investment, which is often reflected in the pricing, so interrogate away. Ask how it deals with stains, if it's available for extra shifts on weekends, and whether it plays well with others. And don't listen to a word suede says, no matter how persuasive; she sure is pretty, but she calls in sick whenever it rains.

Above: Throw pillows can change the look and feel of a neutral-colored couch in an instant. (Picture this same sofa with bright red and yellow pillows to get an idea of what I mean.) In a pinch, throw pillows can also act as floor cushions in a room without a lot of seating.

3 FABRICS THAT HAVE MY SEAL OF APPROVAL

1. LEATHER: One of my favorite options for families is leather. It comes in every style and color under the sun. It can be wiped down and cleaned up easily. And if you go with natural-looking leather, it will age gracefully, embracing scratches and faded patches like a pedigree.

2. SLIPCOVERS: If you're not prepared to commit to leather, slipcovers to the rescue! Not the kind you buy years after your sofa and tuck in around the cushions like a giant sheet—a sofa you buy with slipcovers already in place, designed with zippers and machine-washable fabrics.

Slipcovers are not entirely easy. Be prepared to cart them to your neighborhood Laundromat or dry cleaner if your own machines aren't big enough to accommodate them, and suppress the urge to smooth and adjust the covers as soon as someone stands up. This option is definitely not for the perfectionist.

3. MICROFIBER: People have just as strong opinions about microfiber as they do about wearing white pants after Labor Day. It's hailed by many as the greatest invention in upholstery, a miracle fabric that won't fade, stain, or show wear. However, there are different grades and a wide range of quality in the fabric, which translates to a wide range of user reviews. Is it as impossible to stain and as virtually indestructible as the salesperson might try to convince you? No, probably not (though I have personally seen permanent marker removed from microfiber, so I'm not entirely unconvinced of its miraculous powers). Is it water-repellent and soft next to your skin? Definitely. So follow your couch's care instructions and keep your expectations reasonable, which may mean the pomegranate juice stays in the kitchen and your 100-pound puppy stays at your feet, no matter how he begs . . . because white pants after Labor Day is a stunning style statement—unless it's a muddy day!

05

TEACH YOUR OLD COUCH NEW TRICKS

As the song goes, if you can't be with the one you love, love the one you're with! Just because a new couch isn't in the budget doesn't mean you must resign yourself to a daily groan and wishful thinking every time you walk into the living room. Begin by making a list of everything your couch isn't contributing to your room.

If it's lacking in form, add structure with a sleek, Danish-inspired coffee table or structurally significant side chairs.

Are you missing color and pattern? Throw on a variety of pillows in color combinations that startle your senses a little every time you catch sight of them; you'll forget your couch is even there!

If the couch is too big for your room, add a Lucite table that disappears into thin air. If it's too meager, add weight with a trio of nesting tables.

And before you get too stressed about what your couch is saying about you at this very moment—especially if its springs are not as springy as they once were or its vibrant colors are fading with time—remember that there's something to be said for ugly couches. They can make beautiful childhoods.

Opposite: Note the antique sewing machine on display behind the sofa. It communicates in an instant what sorts of things are valued in this home. The framed maps tell a story as well.

06

VISUALIZE YOUR LIVING ROOM IN SECTIONS

Successfully filling up and arranging one large room can be overwhelming. So once you've decided how you most want to spend your time in your living room, tackle it section by section. Over here is where we'll chat, and there is where we'll read, and that's where we'll play the piano. Like pieces of a puzzle, these sections will become the blueprint of your family time when they're all put together.

One of my favorite sections of our living room is an intimate corner that's easily one of the best spots in the house to have a meaningful, somewhat private chat. Its design is nothing of consequence, really: it's a long bench, against a window looking out onto the trees, with a beautiful lamp close by. But because it's just barely outside of the main gathering space, it instantly feels set apart. So if Maude has a friend over and they'd like to talk

about something that the entire Blair world doesn't need to hear, or Oscar wants to grill his dad about the possibility of being a ninja as a full-time career, we have the perfect place.

Above and opposite: The fireplace creates architectural nooks that are approached as separate sections of the room—one for a piano, one for wood storage. Each looks good in its own right, and the room looks good overall.

07

CLEAR PATHS, CLEAR MINDS: CREATING WALKWAYS THROUGH YOUR SPACE

Is there room to roller-skate through your house? Even if you don't actually own a pair of roller skates, the question is helpful when considering the paths in your home. Try this. Walk from one side of the living room to the other, from couch to chair to bookshelf. Do the same from your front door to your back door. Are there natural paths, or do you find yourself turning sideways here and there and walking around a couch or table to get there? You'll know by a bruised shin if it's time to edit!

When you consider how your family will use a room, don't forget to consider how they'll navigate *through* the room as well. Sometimes, that means flipping every idea you held about how the room— and your entire house—should flow.

Above: A row of three benches underneath a wall of windows keep things light and open while providing extra seating and surface area.

08

LEAVE ROOM WITHIN YOUR ROOM

When I'm designing a layout that works, in addition to our day-to-day needs, I'm also considering seasonal and other decor that will make an appearance every so often. I ask myself where the winter firewood will be stored, where we'll be able to pin the tail on the donkey, where I'll put the hyacinths when it gets too cold outside, where we'll position the Christmas tree, and where we'll hide just before we jump out and yell, "Surprise!"

A living room doesn't need to be crammed full of stuff. Empty spaces don't always have to be filled. I try to remember that the living room, maybe more than any other room in the house, is our family story. It's where we've been and where we hope to someday go. So I always make sure there's a space on the shelves or a spot on the wall for the next memory we'll make. Maybe we'll make it tonight.

Left: An uncluttered room means there's minimal impact when kids come in and out, leaving toys in their wake.

09

FEEL FREE TO ASSIGN YOUR LIVING ROOM EXTRA JOBS

Houses have different duties depending on the family. Yours might need to serve growing athletes, or budding writers, or aspiring actors. We're raising our kids with music lessons, so our living room often doubles as our practice area and concert hall. In my experience, if kids are expected to rearrange furniture, hunt for sheet music, and haul their instruments from the opposite end of the house at practice time, there will be some resistance.

We keep guitar picks in a little bowl near the piano—as soon as the guitar is tuned, you can choose a pick and be on your way. We create storage especially for our sheet music—currently we use a wall-mounted file rack that the music books fit in nicely; in other houses, we've used baskets or bookshelves. And instruments, whenever possible, are displayed as wall art.

It takes some planning and patience, especially when piano and trombone and guitar players are practicing at the same time . . . with different music. Since our living area is open to the rest of the main level, it's important to us to follow a schedule for daily scales. Conversely, the openness of the space allows us to make music together much more easily. If Ralph hears his dad strumming the guitar, he's apt to join in, and there's a good chance the rest of the kids will soon follow. Let's call it the Pied Piper effect!

Opposite: We gave this $500 hand-me-down piano a new lease on life with a fresh coat of (green!) paint, and it now does a great job of making the music area feel friendly and welcoming to kids.

SETTING GOALS AS A FAMILY

Our family keeps a journal where we record our New Year's resolutions, a handy list of goals and daydreams to focus our thoughts when we're discouraged or distracted. To help our kids get started thinking about the coming year, we give them a short reminder about what resolutions are for—to become better people. Then, Ben Blair and I offer prompts to get them started:

THIS YEAR
I want to learn: _____
I want to read: _____
I want to make: _____
I want to visit: _____
I want to be better at: _____
Most of all, I want: _____

The journal is a treasure! It's also a wonderful resource the kids can consult to see how much they're growing and changing. The older kids love to read the resolutions from their early years—here are Olive's resolutions from when she was five.

OLIVE'S 2007 RESOLUTIONS:
I want to learn: ballet, again
I want to read: all kinds of books
I want to make: a Play-Doh horse
I want to visit: Emily D [a neighbor]
I want to be better at: [she couldn't think of anything she wanted to be better at]
Most of all, I want: an Ariel Barbie

Five years old is so cute!

10

REIMAGINE YOUR COFFEE TABLE

All the coffee-table books and conversation starters that reside in your living room need somewhere to rest; a handsome spot in easy reach of the seating.

When rooms are a bit overstyled with furniture you just can't let go of, a Lucite or glass-topped table is almost like an invisibility cloak. Round tables are a refreshing option in a room of rectangles and squares. Upholstered footstools can transform into tables with the addition of a tray when they're not being used for extra seating. And consider casters on your coffee table if your living room is often rearranged, whether for mini dance recitals or get-togethers that spill over from the kitchen.

Above: This coffee table, hewn from a tree trunk, can stand any sort of beating a busy family can throw at it. The round shape means no sharp corners for toddlers to bump into.

COFFEE TABLES THAT WEREN'T BORN THAT WAY

1

STEAMER TRUNKS AND VINTAGE SUITCASES

You can find both of these clever storage solutions in antiques stores or at flea markets. Stack two or three suitcases till you hit the perfect height, or search Etsy for vintage luggage with legs. Or find a steamer trunk worn down within an inch of its life—scrub your treasure, spray it with Febreze if it's musty, and you're good to go. If you don't want to hunt down the perfect antique, you can also choose a modern reproduction from stores like Restoration Hardware.

2

OVERSIZE WOOD BLOCKS

Check with your local lumberyard for rough-hewn industrial-size blocks. Depending on their size, you can stand them up or lay them on their sides. Anything in the 15- to 18-inch range should work. Give them a good sanding to prevent splinters, but otherwise, leave them be and let them gather a natural patina.

3

INDUSTRIAL CABLE SPOOLS

Industrial decor options always catch my eye, and these are the real deal—they come in a variety of sizes, and turned on their sides, they make a handsome table. Find vintage versions on Craigslist or eBay, or do a search for "wooden cable spool for sale" to find sources that sell new spools.

11

A SIDEKICK FOR YOUR COFFEE TABLE

Do you need a side table? Probably. Probably more than one. The coffee table can only take on so many duties. If it's covered in your collection of miniature succulents, there will be no room to set down your magazine. Or if your sofa is long, the coffee table may be out of reach of some seats, and not realistic for holding your cup of tea.

Side tables act as butlers in a living room. They stand at the arm of sofas and chairs, ready to help. They'll hold a lamp to light your pages, or the dog-eared book itself. And some side tables work twice as hard—transforming into stools or storage pieces as needed.

Once you have your sofa and chairs in place, sit with a book, or a glass of water, and it will be easy to see if and where you need a side table. The only real requirement: make sure it's sturdy, and that it won't topple when the room is full of people and one of your kids uses it as a spare chair.

Above: Here, the sidekick comes in the form of a stool, which you can top with a plant or a pile of books, or use as extra seating as needed.
Opposite: Many of the elements in this room—the vintage couch, the embroidered wall art, the pom-pom-edged curtains—look as if they could have come straight from your grandmother's house, but the modern side table, along with fresh white walls and updated throw pillows, makes the whole room feel totally current.

12

COFFEE-TABLE BOOKS AS CONVER-SATION STARTERS

We tend to switch up our coffee-table books regularly, with a blend of hard and soft reads that appeal to each of us personally and those on topics that the world is currently discussing—some serious nonfiction focused on education or human rights, a book all about Wes Anderson, a novel we're reading together as a family, a joke book, and a gorgeous tome or two. There are travel books that are almost as good as a plane ticket, atlases that show us the shape of countries we didn't know existed, and art books that are just as breathtaking as an afternoon at the MoMA. I want the kids to have an appreciation for history and our place in it, so I collect books about ordinary people who do

extraordinary things with their lives. Before a presidential election, there will be two biographies on that table. "Something for everyone" is our book motto, and a quick glance every so often at what we're reading in the living room ensures that we're staying true.

Opposite: Instead of one short stack of coffee-table books, why not fill the whole coffee table? The more books right at hand, the more likely they'll get picked up. And don't be afraid to mix in kid-friendly books with your coffee-table staples.

AT THE BLAIR HOUSE

INSPIRING TRUST AND ENCOURAGING OPENNESS

One of my favorite moments that happen only in our living room is our interviews. Ben Blair and I schedule conferences with each of our children (both parents plus one child at a time) to assess their current state of happiness. We take these appointments seriously, and so do our kids. Whether we're talking about friends or their progress in French, a mysterious pain in their elbow, sibling squabbles, or the pangs of missing old places or old friends, the living room sets the tone that we value the discussion that's happening. It matters, by the very virtue that it's taking place in this room.

We seat the child between us, where we can easily offer hugs. We take notes. Let them speak without interruption. Offer advice and encouragement, and make a list of ways we can help (find a tennis class, replace some holey socks) before we meet again. Ideally these interviews happen monthly, though in reality there are more months where they *don't* happen.

13

DON'T
BE AFRAID
OF ART

It can be daunting to hammer in that first nail to hang a piece of artwork. It feels like such a commitment! But wall decor and artwork can change as easily and as often as your tastes and needs. Nail holes can be hidden, or filled in and painted over and forgotten altogether. So my biggest piece of advice as far as art for your wall goes is, get hanging!

If it catches your eye, if it prompts you to respond to it, if it makes you smile, that's enough to qualify it as "art." Figure out what you love, and don't be embarrassed about it—even if you found it in the discard pile at Goodwill or abandoned in Grandpa's attic, even if it's an inexpensive reproduction made by a student artist, or made by you! The price tag doesn't inform a piece of art's worth.

The artwork can be big or small. You can add many pieces to your walls, or keep them spare. Just start. You're not married to your art. If it turns out you don't like it, you'll take it down. Easy as that.

Above: I really like the sentiment in this framed piece. Growing an art collection is definitely one of those things that should take some time.

CHOOSING THE RIGHT PIECE: 4 PLACES TO START

1. START WITH A FAVORITE. When you think back to your museum visits, or recall your college art history course, is there one image that comes to mind? Perfect. That will look wonderful framed and hanging in the living room! If it was painted by anyone that's even slightly well known, there's a good chance you can buy a print online in any size you like.

2. THINK ABOUT YOUR FAMILY VALUES. Ben Blair and I saw *The Floor Planers* by Gustave Caillebotte for the first time on a trip to Paris early in our marriage and were both drawn to it instantly. To us, it captures feelings of hard work and accomplishment. It reminds us that good old-fashioned manual labor can be transformative. It reflects our family values and would be an ideal choice for our home.

To find artwork that reflects your family values, go to an image website like Art.com or Getty Images and do a search using your value keywords—maybe "compassion" or "loyalty" or "positive thinking." Then see what shows up and pulls you in.

3. CONSIDER HOW THE ROOM WILL BE USED. Artwork can be selected just as you choose furniture and decor—based on how you'd like a room to function. If you want your living room to be a place for conversation, you could choose artwork that starts one, like Picasso's *Guernica* or Frida Kahlo's *Self-Portrait with Cropped Hair*. Or you could be more direct and choose artwork that depicts a conversation, like Paul Gauguin's *Les Parau Parau*.

4. COMMISSION SOMETHING. Collecting original artwork used to be an option for only the upper classes. And commissioning artwork was reserved for the upper, upper classes. But happily, that's no longer true. Talk to the artists in your life, or find student artists at your local university—you can probably make a deal with them that fits your price range.

Tell them what kind of piece you're looking for—what you want it to communicate or how you want to feel when you look at it. Then let them create something just for you. My brother-in-law Paul Ferney is an artist, and as a housewarming gift, he gave us a painting of the home we lived in in France—complete with our vintage Renault parked out front. It's a small painting, 5 by 7 inches, but it's a huge treasure to my family. Having original, one-of-a-kind artwork in the house is a remarkable thing.

MEANINGFUL WORDS POSTER
HAND-LETTERED ART TO INSPIRE YOUR FAMILY

During a particularly challenging period during our home renovation in California, the whole family was feeling discouraged and displaced. The fridge was on the balcony; the kids couldn't access their bedrooms. Everyone was on edge. I noticed a few rolls of blueprints that had been left in the closet when we moved in and used them to make a poster that would remind us that we can do hard things (and hopefully imply that hard things are often worth doing).

Similar words painted on a map might be encouraging during a move, or choose any beautiful paper and make a poster of words that you find important or inspiring. The hand-lettering makes it personal, and one-of-a-kind!

MATERIALS

Scrap paper

Acrylic paint

Paintbrush

Poster paper

STEP 1: Decide on the words or phrase you want on your poster. Using scrap paper, practice hand-lettering the words with the paint and brush. Have different members of the family write the words to evaluate different handwriting styles. Try all capital letters. Try script. Finally, test the paint's thickness on your scrap paper and add water to the paint until the brush achieves a smooth stroke.

STEP 2: Once you're confident with the practice handwriting and have achieved your desired paint thickness, use the main poster background and paint your chosen words. Let it dry overnight, then display it on the wall, framed or unframed.

14

BRING YOUR HEIRLOOMS OUT OF RETIREMENT

Educating your little ones from the outset about family members who came before them is easier with props. Just the simple act of playing with a domino set that was once held by a great-great somewhere far away, both in years and distance, is one of the sweetest history lessons.

Distinguishing between irreplaceable and unforgettable is key. Some of your less breakable items can and should be within arm's reach (and it's good form to make sure even the shortest arms in the house can reach, too).

Vintage toys and well-sealed photo albums, button collections, and books signed by their previous owners are safe to store within reach. Heirlooms like fragile ceramics, delicate linens, and original documents that aren't covered by glass or plastic need to be protected.

Opposite: What people consider heirlooms varies widely. In the case of these images, the objects on display are all tactile, unbreakable, and interesting for kids to interact with.

15

YOUR COOLEST TOYS CAN LIVE IN THE LIVING ROOM

Our living room isn't a playroom, and as a general rule, our toys live elsewhere. But it's a good policy to make a few exceptions. Rather than institute an unwavering No Toys in the Living Room rule—because that's no fun!—proclaim an Only Gorgeous Toys in the Living Room edict. Go through your toys and find two or three of the best-looking ones, then add them to the shelves or side table.

You're looking for nonplastic, design-y toys that are as sophisticated as they are fun. Toys that draw adults in just as easily as kids. Toys that would look right at home on an architect's desk, and that you probably found at a museum gift shop. I favor a basket of wood blocks, painted or natural. A box

of magnetized marbles. A set of building cards designed by the Eames brothers. And a tin of classic dominos.

When your neighbor drops by with her little one, and the visitors migrate to the living room, you'll be so glad you have an instant distraction for the three-year-old, while the grown-ups have a conversation. And if you have a shy or gloomy visitor—young or old—a cool toy will help him relax and clear his mind.

Above: Who would want to put this cute little tractor away?
Opposite: At kid level, these bookshelves offer objects like colorful blocks and a vintage typewriter that little ones will love to interact with. Higher up are toys, like a sculptural bear, that teens or adults can enjoy.

16

START A FAMILY COLLECTION

Someday, your child will be standing somewhere in the world—in an art gallery, on a sandy beach, in the middle of a crowded Moroccan souk, or at a quaint estate sale in the country—and he'll catch sight of a snow globe or an intricate paper cutting or a piece of pale blue sea glass or even a weathered map of a place that will remind him of home. Perhaps it will remind him of you. There might be a tiny gasp as your child time-travels straight back to a shelf in his childhood home where you lovingly kept your family collections.

I think there's something important about the things we choose to pick up and carry through life. Those that we wrap up carefully (and tell anyone who will listen to handle with care!) and move to the next home are more than just mementos. They're a not-so-subtle message to your children about what inspires you.

Years ago, I saw the most brilliant spice rack with tiny glass vessels all lined up, each marked with a place-name and a date. Inside each of those little jars was a handful of rocks or sand or some sort of reminder of where the collectors had walked together.

It was the very best kind of geology exhibit. It was the history of that family. It was magnificent. I'll be honest and tell you my first thought was "Oh no! I wish I had started sooner! I wish I had some of the stones from the black pebble beach we visited in Greece, in the early days of our marriage. And sand or sidewalk from New York." And those pangs of regret stopped me from ever starting that collection.

But you can do better. And you can start now. Really. Empty your old bay leaves—it's been at least two years since you used them. Wash out the jar. Grab your child's hand and head outside. Someday, that backyard dirt and your child's enthusiasm for it will be one of the greatest ingredients in your family memories.

Opposite: Like objects grouped together have more impact. Suddenly they look intentional and are begging to tell their story.

THE KITCHEN

We're all familiar with the saying "Home is where the heart is," but after living in so many homes with so many different features, I'd suggest that home is where the fridge is! In our family, the kitchen is the spot where we do all things food, but it's also the place where we meet in the morning and merge in the evening, where we plan spur-of-the-moment celebrations and last-minute dinners, and hold middle-of-the-night planning sessions when inspiration wakes us from our dreams.

My ideal kitchen can handle all that and more. Its countertops are perfect for teaching the art of making chocolate chip cookies, and the cabinets contain all those magic ingredients that, when mixed together, warm any downcast day—just bake at 350°F for 30 minutes. Glassware, dishes, linens, and towels are always within reach for every table-setter, table-clearer, dishwasher, and dryer extraordinaire. Oh, and there's a spot for music, and many stools for the guests and helpers keeping the cook company.

If that sounds like a lot of duties for one room to perform, it is! Which should make the kitchen the biggest room in any home, right? Not so for a lot of families (mine included), but rest assured, even the smallest spaces can feed your souls. At least three times daily (multiplied by thirty if you've got toddlers).

01

START WITH THE TABLE

For our family, the table has always been key in making our kitchen work. In the smallest homes we've lived in, the kitchen table is where eating, crafting, and heart-to-heart talks happened. Even in homes where we've had the luxury of more space for a project area, the kitchen table is still the most active surface in the house. So choosing a table that we love and that works for our family is at the very top of our list of kitchen needs.

My preference is a surface that looks better with age. Ideally, the table comes to your home with scrapes, dings, gouges, and stains already in place, so that when you add your own, you can feel like you're intentionally deepening the patina instead of sighing over the latest scratch. Consider a decades-old farm table, or perhaps a new table constructed out of barn wood.

Wood isn't the only surface option. Several years ago, we built an oversize table from four-by-eights and fence posts, then topped it with a sturdy sheet of metal that could outlast any mess we might throw at it. (Yes, we throw messes, and yes, the table looks better than ever.) Alternatively, the kitchen table of my childhood was a painted Parsons-style table big enough for my family of ten to crowd around. When the surface became too worn, we just added another coat of paint. All that is to say you're in luck—there are all sorts of excellent options available. I would simply recommend steering clear of anything high-gloss or so high-priced that you'll be tempted to treat it like it's precious. Instead, scour antique shops and flea markets and online garage sales for diamonds in the rough, and give them new life with a weekend spent sanding and staining, or painting.

Opposite: This farm-style table will handle scratches and art projects and just get better with age. The tufted bench on wheels can be rolled to any room in the house as needed.

02

MAKE YOUR TABLE WORK FOR YOU

When considering a possible table, think about the shape. Some spaces lend themselves to a sturdy rectangle; others favor a circle or a square. We didn't try a round kitchen table until we already had five of our six kids, but we discovered that we are big fans. Round tables have a knack for being able to "fit one more person" no matter how many people are already seated. So if you are a family that often finds yourselves with last-minute dinner guests, round tables may work to your advantage.

We've also discovered that round tables seem far and away the best for promoting dynamic family conversations. Maybe it has something to do with removing the proverbial head of the table and making everyone feel equal.

Tables that expand with leaves are also a genius solution to huge gatherings and big family holidays. The farmhouse where we lived in France had a table with simple leaves that took it from a table for eight to a table for twenty-four in a snap!

Opposite: Try mixing different textures and materials. Here, the industrial metal of the table is warmed by honey-colored wood chairs.

03

CHOOSE CHAIRS THAT CAN HANDLE EVERY CELEBRATION AND SPILL

A friend once purchased a set of sturdy rattan chairs for her kitchen. They were crazy affordable—she bought ten!—and all the reviews assured her that they would withstand five-year-olds jumping with glee when butterscotch pudding was served. What no one told her, however, was that they would absorb every spill, every crumb, and every mashed banana in their sturdy weave. Lesson learned: Always choose surfaces that are easily wiped down and sanitized.

During graduate school, Ben Blair and I bought a set of recycled aluminum chairs. They were affordable knockoffs of the famous Emeco Navy chairs, originally built in 1944 for use on submarines and warships. Based on their history, I knew they would be strong enough to withstand the toddler years, while making a strong-enough style statement to pair with anything from a sturdy farm table to a delicate café table. All these years later, those aluminum chairs are still with us. They've migrated from our kitchen table to an outdoor table where they stand up to the weather beautifully.

If metal isn't your style, you could look for wooden chairs with simple lines and fewer crevices for dried food to get stuck in, or sleek modern acrylic chairs that contrast with your farm table in a fantastic way.

Opposite: Mixing yellow chairs in with the white adds a sunny pop of color that accents the black and white kitchen.

04

MAKE SURE THERE'S ROOM FOR ONE MORE GUEST—AND HER FRIEND

More guests mean more joy. They also mean you'll need more dinner table seating options; preferably, ones that don't take up every inch of free space you have in the house when it's just you and your immediate family.

In my childhood home, when there was a particularly big gathering, my siblings and I were sent to the four corners of the house to scrounge up desk chairs, patio chairs, and even the piano bench! At the Blair home, we have guests often enough that we like our extra seating to be close at hand.

Think sleek, stackable stools that lead a double life as side tables or food trays. And how do you feel about benches? I love them. I think I've worked them into the decor of every room in the house over the years. They double as a child-size table or a coffee table, and are strong enough to seat several adults at the dinner table.

Above: A kid-size spot that mirrors the grown-up table is a sweet way to make everyone in the family feel equally at home.
Opposite: This stack of Tolix stools takes up very little space and is ready to offer help as needed—as extra seating, as a nightstand in the guest room, or as a temporary side table next to a sofa.

AT THE BLAIR HOUSE

DAILY FAMILY DINNERS

We believe in family dinners. The kind where we all work together to get plates and forks and drinks and food on the table, and—this is the key—all sit down together to enjoy it and each other for as long as the evening allows. Some of the best conversations in our home happen at dinner, and most meals end with sated smiles on our faces.

Even when one or more of us is out of sorts, there's something restorative about honored family traditions like our shared dinnertime that brings us out of our funk. And when we're all together, I can see more clearly the state of affairs in the Blair family; a quick glance around the table lets me know who's stressed, who's irked, and who's just hungry.

It doesn't happen every night, but our goal is to make dinner together the default. It doesn't need to be fancy or formal; it just needs to be as consistent as possible. Even when we've ordered in pizza and root beer, we'll set the table and gather everyone so we can sit and eat at the same time.

05

CHOOSE DINNERWARE THAT WILL GROW UP WITH YOUR FAMILY

Dinner plates, soup bowls, salad plates. You'll use your dinnerware multiple times, every single day. Since you're going to be seeing and interacting with your dishes that often, it's smart to make sure they're gorgeous and that you love seeing, holding, and using them. Many parents' instinct is to make "unbreakable" the first priority when figuring out what plates will mix with their young children, and so they find themselves in the store aisle filled with plastic and character-laden dishes. But I can promise you there are other options that work for families. Options you'll love even before your kids arrive and after they've flown the nest. Do a little searching and choose dinnerware that's both practical and beautiful. Your choice will make you smile every time you do the dishes.

Above: The open shelves in this kitchen house an assortment of dishes, bowls, and serving pieces that all look right at home thanks to their shared color scheme—a quick way to make a display look thought-out and intentional.

FAMILY-FRIENDLY DISHWARE

1

PEWTER

Long before our kids came into being, we registered for pewter dishes on our wedding registry. (They're actually pewter-*like*; they look and feel like pewter but don't contain lead and are therefore food-safe.) Our thought was that they'd be timeless, unbreakable, easy to move (no extra protective padding required), and as appropriate on a country picnic as at a formal table. They've come in handy during the breakable years and our many cross-country and transatlantic moves, and they still look as good as they did the day we brought them home. And pewter doesn't have to feel medieval—it is available in a surprising number of patterns and designs.

2

ENAMELWARE

I love the look of enamelware. It comes in the traditional specks, but also in a huge variety of painted surfaces. As it ages, the enamel may chip off in a few places, but enamelware tends to have an antique feel, so the chips end up looking appropriate instead of ugly. Enamelware won't last as long as pewter dishes, but it's sturdily made (with metal rims), and the life span is much longer than that of typical ceramic plates. It's also much more affordable than pewter.

3

WHITE CERAMIC DISHES

Yes, they're breakable, but still, I insist on having a set of white ceramic dishes in my stockpile. They're just so practical! Simple white sets with clean lines are readily available at all price ranges. Expect the dishes to break sometimes, but it's easy as can be to find more white dishes to take their place. You can even mix and match your white dishes over the years if you can't find exact replacements. I also love a set of white dishes because when you're entertaining, they can be adapted to all sorts of table decor or holiday color palettes.

06

TO CHINA
OR NOT
TO CHINA

Do you own a set of china? Fine china seems like it has no place in a young family, and yet I'm a fan, and have been since our oldest kids were only toddlers. I don't keep a full set with all the serving dishes and accessories, but I love having china salad plates and dessert plates and teacups and saucers to add to our dishware mix.

My china philosophy has been: Buy an inexpensive but quality option and use it frequently. The pattern in my collection was spotted by my mother on clearance at T.J. Maxx. I swooped in and bought every piece I could afford, and I keep it in an easily accessible cupboard so that we really, truly use it. Yes, we bring it for Thanksgiving dinner and other special occasions, but we also use it on any old Sunday afternoon when we invite friends over for brownie sundaes. It's a subtle creamy pattern I adore. It looks elegant on its own, and it layers with our pewter dishes beautifully.

If you're worried about breakage (and you should be with china, because it *will* break), you have two solid options. The first is to choose a pattern that is easily replaceable. Consider a long-standing china pattern that is either still being produced or was produced so liberally at some point that there is a giant stockpile on china replacement websites. If replacing a specific pattern won't work for you, make it easy on yourself and think outside the pattern. Watch Goodwill or clearance aisles or yard sales for random pieces. Buy two dinner plates in a rose pattern you love, and another one with a metallic gold sheen. Collect a bowl here, a dessert plate there. While a whole set can be very expensive, random pieces sold independently of the whole place setting are a bargain. And a dinner table set with mismatched china is about as charming as it gets.

Opposite: This happy little cupboard makes room for any and all dishes that find their way to the kitchen. Mismatched pieces feel right at home because of the common thread of bright colors, and anything that qualifies can become part of the larger collection.

EASY DIY

"YOU ARE SPECIAL TODAY" PLATE
A NEW FAMILY TRADITION

2

3

4

When I was growing up, one of my favorite family traditions was using our "You Are Special Today" plate. It was a red plate with white script that said, you guessed it, "You Are Special Today." It hung in a place of honor in the kitchen. On birthdays or other special days—maybe we earned a great grade on a chemistry exam or got a personal best at the track meet—we were served dinner on the special plate.

Such a simple thing, but what a treat! We looked forward to our turn with fondness and anticipation, and it always felt so good to be acknowledged in such a concrete way.

MATERIALS

Computer, printer, and printer paper

Scissors

Plate with a blank center

Graphite paper or plain paper

Pencil

Tape

Porcelain marker

Cotton swabs (optional)

STEP 1: Print out the phrase "You Are Special Today" in the font of your choosing, sized to fit in the middle of the plate. Then cut a piece of graphite paper (or create your own by rubbing a pencil across a plain piece of paper) just a bit bigger than your printout. If you like, you can find three designs of the phrase, which you can print out for free on DesignMom.com/book.

STEP 2: Place the graphite paper facedown on the plate. Then place the printout faceup on top of the graphite paper, being sure to center it on the plate, and tape two corners of both papers in place so they don't move around.

STEP 3: Using a sharp pencil, trace the outline of the text, which will leave the graphite tracing on the plate. Then remove the tape and papers, taking care not to smudge the graphite image on the plate.

STEP 4: Use a porcelain marker to fill in the traced lettering. You may want to use cotton swabs to clean up extra graphite smears and/or errors.

STEP 5: Bake the plate according to the porcelain marker instructions to set the ink and make the plate washable. (Typically, 300°F for 35 minutes.)

07

CHOOSE REAL GLASSES AND STEMWARE (just don't make them expensive)

Setting a table with stemware makes any meal feel important—especially to kids. So don't skip the goblets. Instead, keep your eyes open for good-looking, classic silhouettes at a low price point—even better if you can buy them in boxes of twelve at a time. I confess, we don't own any expensive goblets. We liked to set the table with glass even when the kids were very young, and we knew from the beginning that there would be stemware casualties. So we've always kept our stemware simple, and we store an extra box of replacements in the pantry.

If you can't commit to one style of glassware, start collecting. Nothing fancy. Just a few juice glasses and old-fashioned soda glasses here, some goblets there, and a bunch of mismatched stemware scored at flea markets can fill a cup cabinet quite nicely. Scattered on a thoughtfully set table, they catch the light uniquely and add a quirky dimension to your place settings. And no matter what drink your guests request, you'll have the appropriate vessel, which truly is one of the signs of a grown-up home: you have what your family needs, and what your company needs as well.

Above: Touches like this charming little mouse remind family members that "sophisticated" doesn't have to mean "precious."

08

INVEST IN THE STURDIEST FLATWARE

I'll set tables with mismatched dinnerware, and I'll serve drinks out of inexpensive stemware, but I've found I'm a stickler for good flatware. I feel that it's totally worth investing in high-quality pieces. I'm not snooty about brands or materials, and they don't need to be an exclusive pattern. But the utensils should be sturdy and balanced, with a good weight in your hand. If you grab a spoon to scoop some ice cream and it bends, then it doesn't pass my stickler test. Crummy silverware is a bummer.

I still love the pattern we chose when we were first married—it's handsome and heavy and readily available. Pieces are lost from our kitchen now and then, so each year I take inventory, typically in October before holiday gatherings happen, and order replacements. I scoured the Internet to find the lowest price on my preferred pattern, and I keep the site bookmarked. Even when I mix and match my plates, I prefer that all the utensils coordinate. It ties the place settings together, but more than that, it allows me to be confident that all my guests will have high-quality utensils in their hands.

Above: Our flatware pattern is called Old Denmark and it's made by Yamazaki. The pieces have remained sturdy for more than two decades and the look is so classic that two of my siblings chose the same pattern.

09

COLLECT TABLECLOTHS SLOWLY

I adore a stack of ironed and folded tablecloths. As a child, I loved choosing the tablecloth for Sunday dinner. It was the only day we used one, and I would choose carefully, knowing that each cloth brought a certain personality to the table. All these years later, I still think of choosing a tablecloth as a pleasure. We rarely use one for our typical dinners, but we always use one for parties and special gatherings.

Slowly building a collection of pretty linens is a satisfying thing to do. There are new tablecloths in the stores every season. You could choose one as a souvenir from an exotic vacation or hunt down the best one at an estate sale. Though really, you don't need many. I have a tablecloth woven of linen that I inherited from my parents (they bought it on their honeymoon). The color is just off of white and is appropriate for any season. If it was the only one we owned, it would work beautifully for every occasion.

If you are building your own linen closet and thinking about purchasing something beyond classic white, I highly recommend going with red. It works for Valentine's Day, and for patriotic holidays like Memorial Day, the Fourth of July, and Labor Day. It goes well with fall leaves for Thanksgiving, and if you celebrate Christmas, it's appropriate for that, too. It's also good on any old Sunday.

Above: There's nothing like a delicate lace tablecloth to give a table a sense of history. Don't you want to know where it came from and how it was made? (And if it's hard to clean?)

10

COLLECT DISH TOWELS QUICKLY (and often)

While I take my time choosing tablecloths and build up my assortment over the years, I do the opposite with dish towels. I keep my eyes open for good ones—something screen-printed from a favorite Etsy shop or a three-pack of happy stripes I notice on sale—and purchase them several times each year. I try to keep a good stack of new-looking options at the ready, and I don't shy away from ironing them if they need it. We pull out a clean one daily, at least, and when they get permanently stained or start looking faded or sad, I move them to the rag pile and say hello to something bright and clean.

Our current kitchen hasn't been fully updated since the 1980s. It's definitely time for a redo, but

the project has been pushed back while we work on other parts of the house. I'm amazed at how new dish towels—something so simple!—have a way of making the whole kitchen feel fresh and new. I can use them to add color, art, or humor to my kitchen, or to simply accentuate the fact that I just cleaned!

Right: Dish towels as gifts—to give or to receive—are always a winner in my book. There are lots of unique beauties on Etsy, but if I need to pick something up right away, World Market is one of my favorite affordable dish towel sources.

DANCING THROUGH KITCHEN CLEANUP

I think everyone agrees that cleaning up after ourselves is one of those life skills that come in handy on an hourly basis! But if it's never expected, it will never develop. At our house, after-dinner cleanup functions as a mini training session on how to work well as a group and develop a sense of personal responsibility.

We adopted three simple dinnertime cleanup rules from our cousins in Colorado to keep the cleaning flow moving: (1) Never fritter about the edges. If you're holding a broom, you'd better be sweeping and not using it as an air guitar. (2) Find something to do and finish it. If you're clearing dishes, keep clearing until the table is empty. If you're tasked with putting leftovers in the fridge, keep going until all the food is stored. And finally, (3) if you don't know what to do, ask Dad or Mom.

We've found the best way to make it through dinner-time dishes is by dancing through them. Turning on something with a fast-paced, danceable beat gets everyone moving and participating. Make sure you've got music on hand for the occasion, and a way to play it. We keep a small speaker on the pantry shelf and plug in our phones/iPods when it's music time. Over the years, we've created kitchen cleanup sound tracks ranging from big-band marches to the Beatles to Beyoncé. It's a lovely way to learn what's in our kids' ears when they're not listening to us, and a way to introduce our own nostalgic favorites to their repertoire!

Of course, as necessary as shared responsibility is in every family, don't ever underestimate the occasional "Go play . . . I've got this" takeover of chores. An unexpected night off is a welcome treat for anyone and, if we're feeling grouchy, can allow Ben Blair and me to talk out whatever issues are on our minds out of earshot of the kids. Here's a no-fail, get-them-moving playlist to get you started:

1. "Twist and Shout" (The Beatles)
2. "Single Ladies" (Beyoncé)
3. "I Melt with You" (Modern English)
4. "Hey Ya" (OutKast)
5. "I Never Go to Work" (They Might Be Giants)
6. "I Want You Back" (The Jackson 5)
7. "Take a Chance" (ABBA)
8. "Fortunate Son" (Creedence Clearwater Revival)
9. "Empire State of Mind" (Jay Z and Alicia Keys)
10. "Shake It Off" (Taylor Swift)
11. "Diane Young" (Vampire Weekend)

11

MAKE IT EASY FOR KIDS TO HELP THEMSELVES IN THE KITCHEN

To foster independence, we keep plates, bowls, silverware, glasses, and napkins within reach for even the littlest members of our family. Though this sometimes confuses houseguests searching for a cup, it makes it easy for the youngest ones to set the table and empty the dishwasher—by far the most popular chores among the under-eight set.

We also keep the healthiest foods at eye level and within easy reach: a giant bowl of fruit on the counter and nuts, dried apricots, and other nutritious snacks in a kid-level drawer.

Above: Child-size versions of household objects (like this red wooden chair) are a draw for children, and a wonderful way to make your kids feel welcome in their own home.
Opposite: I love this sturdy yellow step stool. Also note the footprint plates lined up on the wall. Such a sweet way to mark the baby years!

12

TEACH YOUR KIDS TO COOK

It's pure magic the first few times your kids turn powder and milk into pudding, watch an egg turn into sunshine on a plate, or flip a flapjack. We start them young in the Blair house, with chopping and mashing ingredients for guacamole and rolling out cookie dough.

We're not aiming for chef status—neither Ben Blair nor I consider ourselves to be outstanding cooks—but we want the kids to be comfortable in the kitchen. The basic goals are (a) knowledge of and acquaintance with common kitchen tools like spatulas, measuring spoons, the blender and mixer, cookie sheets, and pots and pans; (b) familiarity with both cooking and baking recipes (which generally have very different sorts of instructions); and (c) mastery of enough basic meals that they won't go hungry (or broke eating at restaurants) once they move out.

These lessons typically happen during meal prep. Little June (age 4) gets ingredients out of the fridge, while Betty (age 8) stirs the pot of pasta and Oscar (age 10) empties the dishwasher. Olive (age 13) makes cupcakes while Maude (age 15) sets the table. And Ralph (age 17) is the master of the quesadilla, making him our reigning midnight snack maker.

To make the kitchen the "place to be" during meal prep time, we keep the conversation light and silly, set something (like a bowl of almonds and raisins) on the counter to snack on while we work, give assignments to everyone, and make even the littlest ones welcome with sturdy stools and kid-size aprons at the ready.

Opposite: Keeping a play kitchen in the real kitchen (instead of the playroom) means that little ones can mimic your actions all through dinner prep. Note the unique wall organizer as well—taking advantage of unused wall area, this rack eliminates the need for a junk drawer in the kitchen, freeing up valuable storage space.

13

YOU DON'T NEED A GIANT FRIDGE

People assume that with a family of our size, we have the largest refrigerator possible and do all of our grocery shopping at warehouse clubs. Though I do keep a Costco card and use it for all sorts of big purchases, we don't consider Costco our primary grocery store.

At some point, I realized that a smaller fridge, filled with fewer but fresher options, worked better for us. As an example, we used to buy the largest possible jar of mustard in the name of being economical. But as that large jar emptied, the bottom third wouldn't get used. Whether it was because it was too hard to get the product out of the bottom of the jar or because the jar had been around so long that it was grimy and unappealing, family members would open a new jar from the pantry instead of finishing the old one. So I started buying the smaller jar of mustard and, lo and behold, we would use it up before we opened another one.

Before I observed the fewer-but-fresher phenomenon, my fridge was packed. But it was packed with nothing worth eating. Two half-used giant bottles of salsa took up a quarter of the top shelf. An oversize jar of pickles, with only two pickles remaining, was the centerpiece on the second shelf. Big bottles and jars of condiments and salad dressings filled the rest of the space. I'd open the fridge, stare at the packed shelves, and feel like I needed to go to the store.

Now our refrigerator is smaller, and we keep less food in it, but we're far more likely to really eat the food we do have. No doubt this is partly because we can see the food easily on the uncluttered shelves. We're also more likely to buy fresh food. It translates to more frequent but smaller trips to the grocery store or farmers' market.

As I look back, I don't know if this would have worked for us during our "three kids under five" years. But it's something I'm happy we've grown into.

Opposite: In addition to the small fridge, this kitchen is full of unexpected details. An intense red wall. Open shelving made of crates and filled with family photos instead of dishes. Freestanding cupboards made of salvaged wood. A reading lamp on top of the fridge. The whole space is a clear reminder that you don't need permission to break from tradition.

14

YOU MIGHT NOT NEED A MICROWAVE, EITHER

For me, a microwave is a reminder of how small decisions can have big impact. We do own a microwave, but if we didn't, would we buy not-exactly-healthy corn dogs? If we didn't have a microwave, would we air-pop our popcorn instead of buying chemical-laden microwave packs? If we didn't have a microwave, would it force us to slow down certain tasks and add some calm to our routine?

But maybe your family has a favorite comfort food that you cook in the microwave, and you eat it when the kids need help winding down at the end of the day. Or maybe the microwave has really helped foster your kids' independence and they use it to prepare many of their own meals. A microwave might be key for your family.

Consider available counter space, what you plan to cook in the microwave, and how often you plan to use it, and go from there. When we lived in France, our home didn't have a microwave and we got out of the habit of using one. But when we moved to California, we added a small one to an out-of-the-way pantry shelf, and we love it for warming up leftovers.

Opposite: This home's rarely used microwave is accessible without taking up valuable counter space, and it falls below the eye line, keeping the focus on prettier details. Kid-friendly dishes and cups are stored at kid level.

AT THE BLAIR HOUSE

3 RULES FOR TABLE MANNERS

If you've ever taken an etiquette class or read an etiquette book, you know there are dozens of rules and manners that govern fine dining. And if you've had the chance to travel, you know those rules can and do change from country to country. In an effort not to overwhelm, we keep our table manner rules simple, and focus on only three: (1) Chew with your mouth closed. (2) Say "please" and "thank you." (3) Don't reach for food.

We don't drill down on elbows off the table, or napkins on the lap, though we model the appropriate behavior. And if a particularly elegant meal is coming up, we'll review salad forks and dessert spoons. But for typical family meals, the above-mentioned rules keep the table pleasant.

One question you might be thinking: Do we allow screens at the table? We don't really consider "screens down" specific to table manners; it's more just human-interaction manners. But it's not a hard-and-fast rule, because if we're discussing a current event and want to check a fact about it, we'll probably pull out a phone for the few minutes it takes to look up the size of a whale shark.

15

CREATE "WHITE SPACE" IN YOUR KITCHEN

In graphic design school, students are taught to leave white space in their compositions; a place for the eye to rest, and a way to focus attention on the highlights of the page. The same idea works in a kitchen. Keep it simple and enjoy the white space. A half-empty cupboard can be a delight.

I admit that over the years, we've owned a juicer, a bread maker, a waffle iron, an ice cream maker, a panini press, a toaster *and* a toaster oven, an electric kettle, a handheld mixer, and a blender, and I'm sure there are a few more things I've forgotten. The toaster, the handheld mixer, and the blender all earned an immediate and permanent spot in our kitchen. The panini press won us over as well. I approached it rolling my eyes but was surprised to find that we use it regularly. The electric kettle joined our family after we fell in love with an adopted one in France. But everything else has made its way to another home.

Accordingly, we've learned to be more realistic about what we're bringing into our kitchen, appliance-wise. Do we have room to store it? How often do we expect to use it? We generally seem to get by just fine with a blender and a selection of old-school pots and pans that don't require a cord, and the space we've saved in the cupboards and on the countertops by paring down unneeded gadgets can be allotted for something else. Or even better, kept empty.

Opposite: There's a terrific mix of textures and surfaces happening in this kitchen: a sleek modern cupboard next to a salvaged window; a clean-technology dishwasher next to an open-faced cabinet hung with a piece of pretty fabric; and an old-school mixer next to a contemporary piece of pottery to house wooden spoons.

16

GET ORGANIZED (especially behind closed cabinet doors)

Is your pantry tiny? Ours, too. In my daydreams, I picture a walk-in version stocked with bottles of mineral water by the dozen, generous boxes of grains and pastas, neatly stored kitchen appliances that I rarely use but don't want to give up (I'm thinking of you, ice cream maker), a stack of freshly ironed table linens, and a row of raspberry jam jars from the batch I made last June. But in reality, we have a few small shelves to work with.

To make the most of the space, we follow one simple rule when it comes to keeping the pantry and cupboards organized: Make sure everything in the cupboard can be seen. If you put a row of canned tomatoes at the back of the cupboard, and then stack more cans or boxes in front of them, you will not see those tomatoes again for a decade (at which point you will throw them away). It's a

rule I sometimes have a hard time following myself, but there's no escaping it. As soon as an item is hidden, it might as well be in the trash.

The key word to remember is *transparency*. A big part of organization is the ability to see what you've got. In practical terms, this boils down to no overstuffed cupboards, drawers, or cabinets. If you don't have a lot of storage space in your kitchen, then pare down your belongings until they fit the kitchen storage you have. Use the heck out of the items you own, and don't waste cupboard space with stuff you haven't touched since 2008.

Opposite: The key to organization is being able to easily find what you need. In a kitchen, that can mean being able to see all your bowls and tools and kitchen gadgets at a glance. I especially love the pots and pans on a wall (bottom left)—they never fit in the cupboard anyway, and here they look like art.

17

CLEAR YOUR HEAD BY OPENING YOUR SHELVES

Open shelving has a way of making a kitchen feel casual and welcoming in a wonderful way. No need for guests to ask you where to find a glass, because everything is stacked neatly right before their eyes. And those pretty mugs you oohed and aahed over at the ceramic shop? They'll make you smile every time they catch your eye as you walk through the kitchen.

Your shelves don't need to be fancy—from simple boards resting on basic metal brackets to wooden crates mounted directly to the wall, anything deep enough to hold plates or mugs will do the trick. And if your kitchen is full of traditional upper cabinets, you could try removing a cupboard door for a fast refresh with big impact (all you need is a screwdriver!). Maybe start with the one by the sink. Then stack the open shelves with your prettiest dishes or bowls. If you like it, go ahead and take off another cupboard door. And if you want to take it a step further, you can paint the insides of your open cupboards a clean white, or add a pop of color to show off your dishes. Implementing this little trick will bring instant openness to your kitchen. As the space opens up, don't be surprised to find yourself breathing more deeply.

Above: If you're going to go retro, go all the way!
Opposite: Here, under-counter cupboards are hung with a simple sliding piece of linen that hides the less-than-pretty kitchen goods, and can be thrown in the wash when it gets soiled.

18

COUNTER-TOPS THAT FIT YOUR FAMILY'S NEEDS

For those of you who are ready to gut your existing kitchen and start over, let's take a minute and talk about countertops. Kitchen materials are such a personal decision, and they truly can make or break a home. Countertops clearly help determine the look and feel of your kitchen, but they also play a very practical role.

Different families will have different countertop needs. A family that bakes up a storm may prefer a cold, hard surface for rolling out piecrust. A family that does most of their eating out and doesn't care much about the practicalities could pick a surface that's harder to maintain. It can be tricky, getting the perfect countertops for you and yours—and it's often a budget buster. So before you jump into the remodel, think about what makes sense for your family in particular. Create an inspiration board

with materials and ideas that have caught your eye, then cross-reference them with your budget. If funds aren't working in your favor, make a note of ideas that are DIY, or creative solutions like combining two types of countertops salvaged from remnants.

One last bit of countertop advice: If cost is the only thing holding you back—or if you're not yet in your permanent home—consider adding a moveable island topped with your dream counter surface. Or keep a stack of cutting boards cut from your preferred materials to get your fix pretty easily.

Above: Have you ever thought of using two different countertops in the same kitchen? Here, the all-white cabinetry ties them together.

5 COUNTERTOP MATERIALS THAT WORK FOR FAMILIES

1. MARBLE: If the sky's the limit budgetwise, my first instinct is marble. A giant 2-inch-thick slab, *s'il vous plaît*. There's nothing quite like marble. It's perpetually cool and perfect when you're rolling out dough, and it's not afraid of heat, either. It's definitely worth saving up for; it looks elegant and substantial and adds weight and history to any home.

2. STAINLESS STEEL: I happen to have a thing for industrial surfaces, so stainless steel holds endless appeal for me. It looks modern, and it's ideal for those who want their space to evoke the feel of a sleek restaurant kitchen. Stainless steel works for families because it is stain-proof, temperature-proof, seamless, and practically indestructible and reflects light beautifully (but be warned that it will reflect every fingerprint and food smear along with it).

3. BUTCHER BLOCK: One of my all-time dream surfaces is butcher block. In France, the home we stayed in had thick butcher-block counters, and I adored them. Butcher block looks handsome, ages well, and is a soft surface—more forgiving on dropped teacups. It's like a giant cutting board, and you can use it as one. Yes, knives will leave their marks, but if you like the weathered look of wood, that's a plus.

4. CONCRETE: Concrete looks unusual and bold. It's another of those industrial-feeling options that make my eyes light up. If you choose it for your countertops, your guests—and maybe even your kids!—will think you're edgy and hip and have awesome taste in music. You'll love it with kids in the house because it's definitely sturdy and can handle lots of use—just be sure that your cabinets can handle the weight, or opt for a concrete veneer.

5. TILE: Tile is a chameleon. Whether you define your kitchen aesthetic as French bakery, country chic, or bohemian, there's a tile style just for you that fits your budget. I have mixed feelings about tile: I love the look, but I find completely flat surfaces easier to maintain and keep clean. That said, tile is stain-, knife-, and heat-resistant—all good things for the family kitchen.

19

CHOOSE AN ISLAND IF YOU HAVE THE CHOICE

We've had homes with and without a kitchen island, so from experience I can tell you that having one really makes a difference. I like the sort that are business (drawers and cupboards) on one side and leisure (stools or other seating) on the other. In the smallest kitchens, I favor a moveable option—a small island on wheels, with open shelves for storage and a butcher block surface on top, that can be rolled wherever it's needed (or rolled into the hallway if it's not needed at all).

Yes, most of our countertops are installed against a wall, and yes, they are put to good use daily. But there's just something about an island. It allows two people to work across from each other instead of side by side, which means more eye contact and less pressure on someone learning a new kitchen skill—instead of having a parent hover over her shoulder, a child can make her first attempts with the luxury of a little space.

Some of my best memories include family members on stools, chatting with family members in the kitchen, passing mixing bowls back and forth across the kitchen island for taste tests.

My favorite spot for breakfast on busy weekday mornings is a kitchen island as well. Picture some of the kids with steaming bowls of oatmeal, while others are packing a lunch: busy bees, buzzing around the kitchen island.

Opposite: One of the best parts of a counter is the opportunity for cool stools. Here, wood matches wood, but it's also fun to contrast.

20

WALLS ARE MADE TO BE BROKEN (unless they're load-bearing, that is!)

When we bought our current house, the kitchen was functional and had plentiful storage, but there was space for just one cook at a time—and not enough room for our postdinner cleanup dance parties. Instead of chatting with the kids while they set the table and I stirred the Bolognese, I would be alone while all the good conversations were happening on the other side of the wall in the living room and dining area. We decided we needed to remove that wall.

Since it was a three-quarter wall, we knew it wasn't load-bearing, so we felt confident tackling it ourselves. One night after the kids had gone to bed, we just went for it! We emptied out the cupboards and moved the fridge out of the way. Then we took down the cabinets and started dismantling the wall until the work was too loud for the late night. The next day, we finished the loud work with hammers and drills, and hauled everything out. We swept up and surveyed the new space. And it was awesome.

Sure, it was a bit of a construction zone, with issues like exposed wiring, an uncovered vent, and mismatched subflooring taking center stage. But from the very first evening, our family dynamic improved! We could have conversations again and work together much more easily.

It was a major reminder to me of how much design affects us and can alter relationships in a very real way.

Opposite: Using red chairs in this mostly white area draws the eye through from living to dining room, accentuating how open the floor plan is.

21

WHAT ABOUT THE DINING ROOM?

If you've glanced at the table of contents for this book, you may have noticed that there is no mention of the dining room. That's because I'm not a big fan of them, and I haven't met a modern family that they make sense for. A whole room in your house that is used only at dinnertime, and then only if you're not eating at the kitchen table? No thanks.

For decades, the blueprint for the typical American home included space for a table in the kitchen, as well as a separate, formal dining room. That didn't make much sense for the family I grew up in, so my parents turned the dining room into a library with floor-to-ceiling bookshelves. There was still a table in the room—with all the leaves removed to take up the smallest possible footprint—where we could read or study. Then, on those special occasions when we really wanted a dining room, like Thanksgiving or the nights we hosted etiquette dinners for the local youth group, the table could be expanded, the books could be returned to their shelves, and seating could be brought in.

In our homes over the years, if a dining room was part of the layout of the home, we've opted for similar solutions, turning the space into something we'll use daily but that works as a dining room in a pinch.

Opposite: The chandelier, wainscoting, and antique buffet tell us this was indeed once a formal dining room, but instead of being used only for occasional dinners, this space is now put to use at all hours of the day for play, reading, and tea parties.

THE KID'S BEDROOM

When you imagine a child's room, you probably picture a single twin bed, a dresser, a bookshelf, some toys and shoes on the floor—the classic bedroom. But in reality, every family handles bedrooms differently. If you grew up in a big family (like I did), you probably shared a room for much of your childhood. Maybe you're a fan of the family bed and your kids all share a room with you. Or maybe you live in a tiny New York City apartment and your child's bedroom is actually a largish closet.

Or perhaps you've got so much room that all of your kids have their very own sleeping space (whether they choose to stay in it all night or not). A bedroom can be a lot of different things.

When we moved to our place in California, we chose a house with plenty of common space but only three not-that-big bedrooms, and one of those was for me and my husband. Certainly, there was a generous bit of creativity and design involved in figuring out where our six kids would sleep, but as long as the rooms were big enough to hold beds and a bureau or two, we knew we could make it work. And we knew that if we could make the bedrooms feel personal and familiar, the kids would be happy.

Regardless of where your children are currently sleeping or jumping on their beds and asking for another glass of water, right now might be the perfect moment to reimagine your child's room.

01

MAKE IT A *BED* ROOM, NOT A *LIVING* ROOM

Bedrooms, to us, are meant for sleeping. Our only requirements are enough space for a bed and a place to put clothes, with a bedside table and a lamp for late-night reading. Our kids' bedrooms house a few toys and a few books, but the majority of these things are stored in the family room and the living room. Our kids don't even do homework in their bedrooms.

We've lived in several houses over our almost-twenty-year marriage, and every one of them has had smallish bedrooms. So maybe that's how and why our bedroom philosophy developed. Who knows? But essentially it's this: We like it when the kids come out of their rooms and spend time with the family, and that's more likely to happen when all of the "stuff" they're interested in isn't located only in their bedroom.

My advice? Dedicate your bedroom to all things bed, from sleeping to napping to daydreaming. The less there is to do in the bedroom, the easier it is to lure the young ones out, which creates more opportunities for positive family interaction in the shared living spaces. If you want your kids playing board games together while you chop vegetables for dinner, then make sure their bedrooms aren't more tempting than the shared family spaces.

Opposite: Layers are a wonderful way to give a room depth and interest. In this child's room, the bed is layered in front of the curtains, the artwork is layered on itself and in front of the nightstand, and the area rug is layered over wall-to-wall carpet.

02

LET ME TALK YOU INTO A TODDLER BED

The first time you move a child from a crib to a twin bed, you realize that the footprint of a twin bed is huge. And it dwarfs a two-year-old! If square footage is limited, and especially if your child's bedroom is doing double duty as a playroom, I highly recommend going from a crib to a toddler bed instead of straight to a twin. A toddler bed uses a crib-size mattress, but it's low to the ground and doesn't have enclosed sides. Depending on their height, children can use the toddler bed until they're five (or older!).

I know purchasing a toddler bed can seem like a waste of money ("They'll be in a twin bed eventually—do I really have to buy a transitional bed?"), but using one saves so much floor space, it's definitely worth it. We've had two toddler beds, plus a crib, in a small bedroom—and still had space for bookshelves! This would not have been a possibility with two twin beds and a crib. Plus, they look adorable side by side.

And don't worry—toddler beds aren't always race cars, fire engines, or plastic castles. You can build simple platform versions, or choose sweetly designed wooden beds that will last generations. Ours were passed back and forth between families for years!

Opposite: Just because you're using multiple beds in the same space doesn't mean your room needs to be matchy-matchy—just look at these toddler beds with mismatched wood finishes. The very grown-up-looking rug in this child-focused space makes the room feel substantial instead of trendy.

03

DESIGN A ROOM THAT WORKS RIGHT NOW

I've never subscribed to the "someday" school of decorating. Cribs that magically transform into daybeds, or that can be reconfigured to fit a full-size mattress, hold no value for me. I can't think of anything I've purchased for my toddler with the hope that he or she will use it into adulthood. I've found life to be too unpredictable for purchases like that. A bed frame that made sense in one house might be too tall for the bedroom windows in the next.

The same goes for designing your entire home. I wholeheartedly discourage you from making or postponing design decisions with resale value or your future wish list in mind. Design your house so that it works for your family right now. And then make adjustments as you go along. If and when it comes time to move on, you can make changes if necessary. But it would be a shame to live in a home surrounded by design decisions you've made for its future owners. Plans change and a temporary stay in a home can turn into years, so do what you can to love whatever house you've turned into your home.

Opposite: So much fun stuff in this room! I especially love the oversize task lamp, the lion mask, and the giant furry throw rug.

04

ABOUT BUNK BEDS

Bunk beds are genius when it comes to space-saving—if I had tall enough ceilings, I'd be tempted to build bunks right to the roof! They seem like they would be the natural choice for any kids sharing a room, but our family has learned from experience that bunk beds work better in some houses than others, and they work better with some ages than others as well.

We favor bunk beds for the five- to ten-year-old crowd. If your child's eyes light up whenever she spots a bunk bed at the store or at a friend's house, and if she starts playing rock-paper-scissors for the top bunk, you'll know that bunks are a good fit. But once your child starts staying up later—say, during middle school—that top bunk loses its appeal. Having to drag herself up the ladder late at night becomes irritating instead of charming. And the lower bunk is no help either, because as your child gets taller, sitting up in the lower bunk becomes a problem. Even though the mattress on your bunk bed is the same size as the twin bed they'll use in their future college dorm, you may find that your kids age out of bunks.

Room size or ceiling height can be another bunk bed deal breaker. Though a bunk bed saves floor space in a small bedroom, if the ceiling is standard height or lower, it can overwhelm the small space and make the whole room feel out of whack. That's what happened to us in the boys' room when we first moved to California, so we switched to two twin beds instead.

On the upside, if your room feels spacious, and your kids are in the right age range, bunk beds get a huge thumbs-up from me and from kids everywhere. They can really feel quite magical. It's like sleeping in a fort! An inexpensive wooden set, painted in a cheery color, is a bold statement that you can design a whole room around.

Opposite: These bunks are an inexpensive wooden set from Ikea, made distinctive with a coat of red paint. And did you know that wall maps come in wallpaper form? It makes for a bold background that works in the bedroom, playroom, or family office.

ON SIBLINGS SHARING A BEDROOM

As one of eight siblings, I shared a bedroom for most of my childhood. In college dorms and apartments, I shared bedrooms with roommates. And I have shared a bedroom with my husband for the two decades since our wedding. So sharing a bedroom seems totally normal to me. But if you grew up with your own bedroom, or wishing you had your own bedroom, the whole concept may seem unrealistic or unacceptable to you.

If you find yourself in a situation where your kids are stuck with sibling roomies and they're not happy about it, let me offer some comfort: It will all work out. Shared bedrooms are a reality for millions of families.

We've had two kids in a room, three kids in a room, even four kids in a room over the years. We've had sisters and brothers in the same room. We've had a baby and a tween in the same room. We currently have a junior in high school and a fourth grader in the same room. There's always a way to make it work, I promise.

It's not magic; it just takes some problem solving. Observe the new roommates' reactions (and possible complaints) for the first week or so after room sharing begins, then address the issues that arise. There are so many creative ways to figure this one out. You can institute separate bedtimes. You can add curtains or bookshelves as room separators. You can create other "getaway" spaces in your house like a reading nook or a porch swing where your kids can go for alone time.

Or you might adopt our bedroom philosophy: Move the toys and books and homework to the family room, and remind yourself that it's okay if children's bedrooms are simply for sleeping. (Because hey, if they're asleep, they can't be bothered with whether or not their sibling is sleeping in the same room!)

05

SIMPLIFY YOUR BEDDING

"Ninety percent of a clean bedroom is a made bed." Have you heard that piece of advice? In my experience it's absolutely true, and I've tried hard to teach this bit of wisdom to my kids. I also help my kids out by keeping the bedding simple. Yes, layered quilts and comforters and top sheets and shams make for the prettiest beds, and as your kids get older, feel free to pile on the throw pillows. But while they're little, less is more.

A trick to help you help them: Skip top sheets, which are difficult for many young kids. Use a duvet cover over a comforter insert instead. When you wash the fitted sheet, throw the duvet cover in the wash as well. And don't feel an ounce of guilt about it. Every European hotel I've ever stayed in uses a duvet instead of a top sheet. It's totally legit.

Above: Making a crib is as easy as it gets. Skip the dust ruffle and bumper pad—all you need is a fitted sheet and one blanket, folded or hung over the side rail.
Opposite: Extra pillows displayed at the foot of the bed give this standard twin a daybed feel.

06

KEEP AN EXTRA SET OF CLEAN SHEETS ON HAND

Washing the bedding is a big chore at our house, and my instinct is to put it off as long as possible. To take the sting out of it, I keep an extra set of clean sheets in a basket under each bed (or in the bedroom closet or a dresser drawer). When it's time to change the sheets, the kids and I can quickly strip the beds and make them up with the clean set from under the bed. Then I can take my time doing the washing. Tomorrow. Or the next day.

By keeping an extra set of sheets in the rotation, you won't have to beat the clock to get the sheets laundered, dried, and back on the bed before bedtime. Bonus: This trick is also helpful for those middle-of-the-night accidents.

Above: Before you send your grandma's afghans off to Goodwill, check trend-making stores like Anthropologie to see if they're carrying something similar—just like everything else, styles of linens and blankets go in and out of style.

07

MAKE ROOM FOR YOUR CHILDREN'S GUESTS

For hosting sleepovers or visiting cousins, or for those nights when all the siblings want to camp together in the same room, we use roll-up Japanese futons. Unlike the couch versions you might be envisioning, these futons are made to roll out on the floor. When daytime arrives, simply roll them up again and secure them with self-ties, like a sleeping bag. Then back in the closet they go.

Though they move from room to room easily, we don't take these futons camping or to slumber parties. They're substantial enough that they're actually comfortable—which makes them a little cumbersome.

Above: We love these mats! We have three and put them to use often.

08

A NO-DISTRACTION NIGHTSTAND

I always prefer side tables to be uncluttered, especially the ones next to our beds. My formula for kids' nightstands is pretty simple. First, if the surface area is small, move the lamp. Instead of a table version, choose one that can be mounted to the wall or attached directly to the headboard. The table should hold a favorite book to read together, a book to read independently, and a journal and a pen to document great dreams and big ideas that come only late at night or early in the morning. Making room for a glass of water makes good sense as well. And there should be space left over for a note from the Tooth Fairy or the plastic figure your child won at the carnival. Keeping the nightstand clear of clutter lets the books and tiny treasures get all the attention.

You may notice I didn't mention a place for an iPod. And that's because we prefer to keep electronics out of the kids' rooms. Especially at the end of the day. We gather the personal screens as we make the bedtime rounds, then bring them to the charging station in the master bedroom, where they stay until the next day. It's incredibly hard for some kids to resist spending a late night with their favorite apps when the screen is right there on the nightstand.

Opposite, clockwise from top left: When it comes to nightstands, you've got options. You can go with a sweet little stool, a small bookshelf that can hold a car collection, something traditional, or an old crate standing on its end that can hold even the tallest picture books.

09

PUT CLOTHING WITHIN EASY REACH

Clothing storage solutions for your kids are going to change with every age. As soon as your children graduate from tiny hangers and baby socks, they'll want to reach their favorite shirts and pants on their own, sometimes several times a day! Determining how much is reachable is the key.

For toddlers, keeping a select few clothing options in low drawers, or in open baskets on the closet floor, allows them to choose their own clothes—sort of. When kids get older, say ages seven to eleven, put a hanging rod at half the closet height, so they can easily reach it and learn to hang their own clothes. And as soon as they're teens, make sure there's space on the floor for the pile of clothing they will shed without a second thought. In all seriousness, hangers actually help older kids who find themselves in an "I have nothing to wear!" fit, because most everything they could wear is in plain view.

No matter your child's age, make a habit of keeping dresser drawers no more than halfway full. When they open their drawers, your kids need to be able to easily see everything that's in them, without shifting things around. If they're overstuffed, they become completely dysfunctional.

Keep what they wear right now handy, and use out-of-reach spaces to store what they don't wear at the moment. Install a shelf at the top of the closet to store off-season clothes, and keep a stool or stepladder nearby (maybe even in the closet) so you can reach the upper shelf when you need to.

Opposite, clockwise from top left: A kid-size clothes rack (to make your own, attach galvanized pipe pieces to a painted plywood board, then add wheels); two low dressers that provide ample, reachable clothes storage for little kids and can be split apart if you want to reconfigure the room; a closet with doors removed, fitted with toy shelves and a hanging rod set at preschooler height; open shelving, perfect for a baby's room.

10

INVENT
A CLOSET
IF YOU
NEED TO

We are no strangers to bedrooms without closets. It happens. Especially if you're living in an older home. In the very first home we bought, when we had only two little ones, we converted attic space into bedrooms, and there was no closet to be had. When we were in France, we lived in a home with five bedrooms, and not one had a built-in closet. In our current home, we've turned what was a small den into a bedroom. Once again, you guessed it, there are no traditional closets. If you find yourself in the same spot, you may need to get creative in order to deal with the clothes storage. With daily clothes changes, pj's, sports uniforms, and games of dress-up, clothes can mess up a room like nothing else. So finding a solution is essential.

Happily, you've got options—including the original bedroom closets, armoires. In fact, that ancient house we rented in France had an armoire in each bedroom. With a hanging rod and shelves

hiding inside, they are perfectly charming and functional. They come in all shapes and sizes, and there are versions that can look the part in both modern and traditional homes.

Above: I'm such an armoire fan. I love that this one has mirrored doors to make it work even harder.

CLOTHING STORAGE BEYOND THE ARMOIRE

1 SIMPLE DRESSER

When kids are young, they may not need hanging space at all. In that case, a simple dresser could provide all the storage necessary. Socks and underwear in one drawer. T-shirts and jeans in another. And pajamas and swimsuits in a third. If drawers don't make sense for the space, the same idea could work with baskets on a bookshelf.

2 INDUSTRIAL GARMENT RACK

Why not show off your teen's budding style? Try an industrial garment rack (maybe one with wheels!) along a blank wall in her bedroom, right next to a full-length mirror. She can hang all her Forever 21 scores out in the open, and mix and match outfits to her heart's content. And if the rack is looking bare, it's a visual reminder that it's time to throw a load in the washing machine.

3 OUT-OF-THE-ORDINARY CLOTHING DISPLAYS

This is one of those design moments that can affect the room's entire personality, so don't be afraid to think up a solution that doesn't seem very closet-like at all. Some of the more imaginative clothing display options I've seen range from a ladder hanging from the ceiling to a sturdy rope strung from one side of the room to the other. Somehow, having clothes on display and arranged by color or style leads to a more well-edited wardrobe. And that's something we can all strive to achieve, right?

11

MAKE A SEASONAL SWITCH

The first snowfall of the season, and you realize your daughter's snow bibs are several inches too short. It happens to the best of us. So take an afternoon to go through the kids' closets when the weather warms up around May, and again at the end of the summer. Donate what they've outgrown, or store it for a younger sibling. Put the off-season clothes in a bin, or basket, or box, and place it on the top shelf of the closet.

This is the time to not only switch out seasonal clothing but also take inventory and make a note of what your kids need. A new hoodie, two pairs of wool socks that will work with boots, a pair of jeans in size 8. Then keep the list in your handbag (or on your phone) and you'll be ready the next time you find yourself at the mall or browsing your favorite online shops.

Storing off-season clothes also means a less-crowded, easier-to-navigate closet. Kids will be able to find what they need quickly, and it will be simpler for them to put their clothes away on laundry day.

Opposite: Things I love about this closet: The hanging rod is within reach of the child who sleeps in this room, and it's not overstuffed, so it's easy to see what's ready to wear. There's no door (aka nowhere to hide a mess), which means there's incentive to keep things simple and organized. Lastly, there's plenty of space—and storage—for off-season clothes and still-growing-into-them clothes.

12

DON'T HIDE THE HAMPER

Hampers hidden in closets or behind doors don't get the attention they deserve. The phrase "Out of sight, out of mind" isn't as calming a thought when it comes to kids' dirty laundry! Keeping the hamper in full view gives dirty socks and underwear the greatest possible chance of making it inside, instead of on the floor.

And don't feel like it has to be a plastic laundry basket. Handsome hampers used to be nonexistent, but now they're easy to find. And really, any container that's simple to empty and fill and won't snag or stain your clothes can become a hamper.

Right: A stylish hamper adds a fun design element to this light and bright shared room.

HANDSOME HAMPER ALTERNATIVES

GALVANIZED METAL WASH BINS

I originally started buying these round metal bins at the hardware store to use as a place to corral ice and sodas during backyard barbeques, but I quickly realized how versatile they are. I love old-school metal bins as a hampers. They seem to fit especially well in a room that has some rustic or industrial touches. Out in the open, they look cool, and the wide opening is easy to throw dirty clothes into.

OVERSIZE WOVEN BASKETS

Anytime I'm running an errand that takes me to T.J. Maxx or Ikea or World Market, I check out the basket options, keeping my eyes peeled for anything unusually good-looking. They can be put to a million uses, and I like to have several in the house. In the bedroom, big baskets can be hampers, a spot for stuffed animals to congregate, or a place to toss throw pillows at night.

INDUSTRIAL LAUNDRY BINS

Over the last decade, there has been a resurgence of industrial laundry bins. Often made of wire, and sporting wheels, they sometimes even have compartments for sorting lights and darks. They're intended for the laundry room, but they're good-looking enough that I favor making them obvious in the bedroom instead. Then, on laundry day, they can be rolled right to the washing machine.

13

HANG A MIRROR, MIRROR ON THE WALL

Mirrors play a huge role in our lives. Babies see themselves in them for the first time and are mesmerized. Toddlers learning to talk can babble for hours, and their reflections always understand perfectly. And don't you remember trying out dance moves as a teenager, or just admiring yourself?

Mirrors are part of growing up, and they teach us a lot about self-awareness, so keep a full-length one in your child's bedroom. And if there's a part of the room that has flattering light, place the mirror there to take full advantage! Dreamy light filtering in when your daughter snaps a selfie of her first-day-of-school outfit? Check.

Above: When hanging a mirror in a little kid's room, get on your hands and knees so you can see the room from her perspective. It needs to be almost to the floor if you want her to be able to see her toes in it.

14

ADD A DOSE OF WHIMSY

If I were a kid again, I'd love it if my mom turned my closet into a hidden escape just for me. I try to remember that desire for whimsy when I'm decorating for my own family. Ask yourself if you need the entire closet for clothes storage, or if you can dedicate that space to something unique, even temporarily. Add a canopy of gauzy fabric above the bed, or wrap a string of twinkle lights around the bars of the footboard. Hang a flock of origami birds from the ceiling. It doesn't have to be fancy, expensive, or difficult, but the little bits of magic you create in your children's bedrooms make for memories of an enchanting childhood.

Above: Whimsy can mean lots of things, but hanging objects (like this gauzy fabric) are often good contenders. Other options include garlands, mobiles, paper airplanes, origami cranes, and your favorite kite.

15

HELP YOUR CHILDREN TREASURE THEIR TREASURES

As much as I like bedrooms to be sleep-only zones, there are certain objects that just don't make sense in any other room in the house. Like the collection of pebbles that your daughter finds on her daily walks to school, or the pennies from foreign lands that your son's aunts and uncles bring as souvenirs.

With that in mind, think about where your kids will keep their treasures. The hideaway can be small, medium, or large—the size is less important than the fact that it's there and it's theirs. Give them a pretty box to decorate, and instruct them to fill it with whatever they love. Choose a nightstand with a little cupboard ready to house small odds and ends. Or put a trunk at the end of their bed, something big enough to compile the treasures over the years—first feathers they found at the park, then scribbled love notes in third grade, then trophies from rec league soccer.

Above and opposite: Little cupboards, tin lunch boxes, mini suitcases, display boxes, small drawers. Even in shared rooms, it doesn't take much to ensure that each child has his own special place to stash his favorite things.

16

SPOTLIGHT YOUR CHILD'S INTERESTS

While putting their room decor together, it's possible to encourage your children's interests without feeling like the whole room has devolved into a tacky mess. If your daughter wants to be an astronaut when she grows up, paper one wall of her room in giant printouts of NASA's spectacular photos from space. (Hint: You can download them for free because they're in the public domain.) If your son is passionate about skiing, look for historic travel posters featuring world-famous ski resorts.

Or skip installing wall art and let them make their own. Pick a wall in their room that can be graffitied. Attach a can of markers to the wall and let your kids have at it. They can mark their height. Doodle. Trace favorite drawings. Write messages. Sign their name. Visiting friends can make their mark as well. Over a year (or two or three) the wall will fill, then get covered with a new layer of drawings as your kids draw right over the old sketches, notes, and signatures. Can you imagine if your parents had done this for you? Mind-blowing!

And if a free-for-all wall is too out of control, you can always go with a more traditional solution like a bulletin board (turn the page for my DIY version). But do it in a big way: Put one in an oversize frame. Or cover a door. Or a whole wall. Within three days, it will be papered with the heartthrobs or rock stars du jour, plus ticket stubs and the coolest logos from the latest coveted brands. Maybe a college pennant from a dream school or a flag from a dream destination. Picture Ferris Bueller's room: More is more.

Opposite: Make your own custom "wallpaper" with a collection of photographs capturing a theme, like cool cars you and your child have spotted on your walks to school, or the prettiest sunsets. Every time you have ten or so good ones, have them printed out and attach them to the wall with putty or double-sided tape. You'll be surprised by how fast the collection grows.

FABRIC-COVERED BULLETIN BOARDS
BIG OR SMALL, THEY WORK IN EVERY ROOM

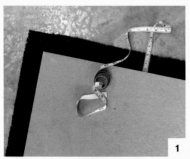

For this project, you'll need to buy a sheet of Homasote. You'll typically find it in 4-by-8-foot sheets near the plywood and insulation at a hardware store (it's made for soundproofing), or you can order pieces online.

For the biggest impact, keep the sheet at full size and lean it against the wall, floor to ceiling. Or cut it into smaller pieces and make a bulletin board for every room in the house. It's easiest to get the Homasote cut at the hardware store, but I've also cut it myself with a utility knife and a straightedge.

MATERIALS

Homasote

Fabric of your choice (enough to cover the Homasote—avoid patterns with straight lines, which can be hard to keep straight when stretching across the Homasote)

Staple gun

⅜-inch staples

STEP 1: Place the fabric facedown with the Homasote on top. Cut the fabric 2 inches bigger than the bulletin board on all four sides.

STEP 2: Staple the fabric three times in the center of one side. Then pull the fabric taut on the opposite side and add three more staples. Repeat on the remaining two sides. Continue making your way around the bulletin board, working from the center of the sides toward the corners, pulling the fabric tightly and stapling as you go.

STEP 3: At the corners, fold the fabric as if you're making the bed or wrapping a present, then staple it down. Now you're ready to add pins, staples, needles, tacks, or whatever you have on hand. They will hold firmly in the Homasote and you can hang jewelry, little canvases, sunglasses, a medal from the track meet, or whatever you like.

DEALING WITH DISNEY

We are Disney fans. We love Disney Parks. We have spent many happy evenings testing each other on Pixar movie trivia. And we have all the lyrics to the *Frozen* sound track memorized. But I have been quite strict about keeping the associated character paraphernalia out of the house. We flat out don't do character bedding or room decor. We are adamant about no character clothing or shoes. And with few exceptions, we've avoided character toys. But at the same time, we've maintained our love for current movies and popular kid stuff.

When your son falls in love with *Finding Nemo*, encourage sea-life exploration with good-looking scientific charts about sharks, a family pass to the aquarium, and an ocean-themed birthday party. When your daughter's eyes light up at the sight of Buzz Lightyear, print NASA's photos of space as oversize posters, make papier-mâché models of the planets, and embroider constellations on a throw pillow for her bed.

It's 100 percent possible to make a room your child will love without involving Olaf the Snowman bedding. You are a creating a home, and you have the right to draw lines about what you will and won't allow in the house. You should be intentional about the atmosphere you are creating.

My last bit of advice on this topic: If your daughter needs new shoes, and you know she'll make a big fuss when she sees the Elsa sneakers, simply don't take her to the store. Save that errand for online shopping, or a late-night Target run. If she doesn't know that Elsa sneakers were an option, she won't feel like she's missing out, and whatever new shoes she does end up with will feel like a fun surprise.

THE FAMILY
ROOM

Family rooms first came into being around the 1950s. If you're living in a house that's older than that, your living room may be doing double duty as the family room—and perhaps the playroom as well. Regardless of its name, this room wears a lot of hats. This is where we relax. It's where we watch TV. It's where the toys live. And it's where much of our home library lives as well. It's not a room designed for deep conversations, though sometimes they happen there anyway.

The family room is expected to accommodate the at-play needs of all of my kids, from teen to toddler, which means it's the place where Ralph, Maude, and Olive can have a lip-sync contest while Oscar and Betty play with Legos and June takes apart the puzzle she just put together. The family room is designed for the whole family.

01

A SOFA YOU CAN SINK INTO

At the Blair house, you can find the coziest sofa in the family room. I resist sectionals in the living room because their unusual shapes aren't very flexible, but I favor them for that prime spot in front of the TV. Yes, I still insist on handsome proportions and fabric that practically invites you to sit down, but comfort is equally important here, if not more so. In the family room, I want a sofa that fits everybody. I look for models that are deep enough for snuggling, with cushions I can sink into a little bit—something with some give. And I keep the throw pillows to a minimum to avoid crowding the needed seating room.

I've dared to order living room couches online without first testing them in person, but for a family room sofa, in-store testing is key. Sit on the floor model. Try lying down. See how it feels when several of you are sitting on it. Try jumping on it or doing a belly flop (just kidding—don't do that). Is it comfortable when your son wants to lean on you for a back scratch? Would your daughter be fine to lie there all day, watching old episodes of *Little House on the Prairie,* when she's home from school with a fever? If the answer is yes, you've found a winner!

Left: A side table turns into a play table with the addition of a kid-size chair. Opposite: This orange-velvet couch likely had a former life in a formal living room, but old, no-longer-pristine velvets retire wonderfully in family rooms.

02

EXTRA SEATING WITHOUT EXTRA CHAIRS

Even if we're having only a couple of visitors, we run out of couch space fast. And there will never be a couch big enough to fit the entire high school track team when we decide to host a karaoke party. But I've found that a "Princess and the Pea" stack of floor cushions solves the problem in a snap.

They add extra seating to any floor and can turn your family room into a fort for the six-year-old's playdate within seconds. They can be moved to a quiet corner when someone wants to curl up with a book, or used as a stage when the youngest sings "Tomorrow" again. Best of all, they are available in patterns and colors to fit whatever style you're going for.

Above: These rattan floor cushions are so practical you'll wonder how you lived without them. Stack them as a footstool or a makeshift coffee table. Use them indoors or out. Spread them out as extra seating in a full room. The simple texture would look good almost anywhere.
Opposite: If you can work a hanging chair into your home, I say go for it. It's instant magic.

03

FURNITURE THAT MOVES AS QUICKLY AS YOUR KIDS

When you're designing the family room and selecting furniture, your primary concern is going to be comfort. But if you're asking your family room to take on several roles, furniture that moves easily is a big bonus. Imagine a coffee table that rolls to the side to make space for gamers to maneuver. Or lidded toy bins that can stack easily in the hallway when more sleeping-bag room is needed. Or a play table with folding legs that can be rested against the wall during fort building. We like our family room to be flexible so we can rearrange it on the spot to make way for a slumber party, a jam session, a club meeting, or a movie screening.

Above: This DIY rolling sofa is so simple, it's genius. Paint storage pallets and add wheels and cushions and voilà! As a bonus, it can double as a guest bed.
Opposite: A clean, neutral room gets a personality upgrade with this salvaged wood coffee table and graphic curtains.

CREATING A MOVIE PARTY TRADITION

There are a few easy and fun things we do to make our movie parties feel amazing. First, we pull out our dedicated popcorn and treat bowls—they're nothing fancy, but because we use them only for movie nights, they're automatically special.

Next, we make a bigger-than-usual effort with the treats. We might pop a bowl of popcorn on any old night, but we upgrade it for movie night. We'll flavor the popcorn or pick up our favorite movie candy. This is really just a tiny errand—it's not like I'm mixing three different-colored frostings for handmade cookies. But a little effort goes a long way.

We also make a habit of wearing pj's for movie parties. The whole family—from June to Ben Blair—changes into something comfy. This isn't something we do on an average screen-watching night, but we instituted the tradition for movie parties to further set the evening apart.

Lastly, we like to start our family movie parties with a bang. So before we press PLAY, Ralph does a little fanfare on the trombone. I realize that you probably don't have a horn player on hand. But once upon a time, neither did we—instead, we'd start things off with a family cheer. Something as simple as "Rah! Rah! Rah! Blaaaair Movie Night!"

Putting in this extra effort may seem like no big deal, but here's the thing: This is the stuff that makes for cherished family memories. I mean it. If you put on special movie parties, even two or three times a year, as adults your kids will remember it like this: "Oh, man! We had major movie parties! Every weekend! It was awesome!"

04

DON'T HIDE THE TV

There have been times and houses where I've tried to hide the TV, but I got to a point where I felt like it was silly to hide it. I don't know the stats, but my guess is that 99.9 percent of American homes have a television. So I recommend being realistic about it, and planning for it as you put your room together. What's the best TV wall? Where will people sit to watch it? Can you see the screen clearly from every seat on the couch?

Once you know where you want to display it, think about what else might be around it. You can make a space for it among bookshelves. Or you could make it part of a gallery wall. In the house I grew up in, the TV was in front of a wall-size map of the world, and my siblings and I grew up with random bits of geographic knowledge from staring at the map during commercials.

Now that laptops and tablets allow us to make any room a TV room, our home has only one actual television. We mounted it on the wall in our family room, but we haven't used it as a traditional TV in many years! We depend on services like Netflix and Hulu Plus and Amazon Prime and Apple TV to watch exactly the show we want, exactly when we want to, pausing or rewinding as needed. It's a different world. My kids will never know the thrill of just barely and breathlessly making it to their spot on the couch seconds before the opening scene of their favorite show.

With the advent of portable screens, why have a TV at all? I find we still put our family-size screen to good use. We use it to surf the Web as a family, looking up a YouTube video that will make everyone laugh. We use it for movie parties and to watch big games or our favorite awards shows. We use it to play Wii tennis and Dance Dance Revolution.

Opposite: There's no pretense of hiding or camouflaging the TV cord behind a plant or a piece of furniture here—it's enclosed in an on-the-surface metal guard. The exposed metal lends a nice industrial touch to the exposed brick.

FAMILY SCREEN TIME & SOCIAL MEDIA

The Internet is now a major part of our lives and our world, and we're deliberate about how we welcome it into our home. We've instituted a tradition we call "Family Screen Time," built not around the TV but around the many small screens we have: smartphones, iPods, a Kindle, and an iPad.

We gather together, get comfortable on the sofa, and simultaneously watch screens and interact with one another. During a typical Family Screen Time session, Ralph and Maude might be sharing music and weighing in on a new band one of them just found, Olive might be asking me if I've seen the latest photo she's posted to Instagram, June and Betty could be watching a movie on a shared iPad, and Oscar might be helping his dad consider edits on an Olive Us video. Screens are passed around. A note is sent to Grandma on Facebook. Everyone is together. Everyone gets to see what everyone else's screen interests are.

The only rule? No headphones. Yes, that means lots of sounds might be happening at once, but the point isn't to have concentrated screen time, or to mark tasks off a to-do list. Family Screen Time is an excuse to have everyone in the same room, interacting with each other, and using the screens to facilitate the interactions and let everyone take part.

Of course, I get it when others suggest that social media is negatively affecting family relationships. But in my own life, the opposite has happened. We don't live near all our friends and family, and we see those dearest to us maybe once or twice a year if we're lucky and organized. It's social media that connects us all so easily.

We've arranged Facebook groups where aunts and uncles can talk to nieces and nephews, and we have Sunday night online gaming sessions that take place simultaneously in three different states. When Ralph was in England and Olive was in France, we could all share a screen at the same time with a Google Group Chat. Of course, there is a risk that any tool can be ill-used, but there is also a real benefit to learning how to use a tool in a responsible way and to make it work for you. In our case, social media is the key to maintaining our faraway relationships, so I'm grateful for it.

05

TOY STORAGE: EASY TO FIND, EASY TO PUT AWAY

Toys can take over a room. So figuring out storage that will work for both you (looks great!) and your kids (easy access!) is the goal. Any furniture store you walk into will have a toy storage system to offer—probably a dozen. But before you take the plunge and invest in one, sit with your room for a while and see how it's working. What toys are being played with in which corners of the room? Should all the toys be stored together? Should there be a basket for dolls by the play kitchen? Should the Legos go in one giant bin, or in several smaller ones, where they can be sorted? Should board games be stored by the other toys, or near the coffee table, where they are more likely to be used?

Think hard about cleanup, and make it as easy and simple as possible. So easy the three-year-old can do it, and so simple that it will make sense, with no explanation needed, to any babysitter you hire. Sort the toys into bins/boxes/shelves by kind, and make their contents identifiable. You could try transparent bins, or add labels with little illustrations of what goes inside. Or you could color-code—Matchbox cars in the red bin, My Little Ponies in the yellow bin. And don't overfill them—leave some space so your kids can grab the toy they're looking for without having to dump out the whole basket.

Then, consider age-appropriate access. Put the baby toys in a basket on the floor that can be discovered by an adventurous crawler. Put the Duplos within easy reach of the preschooler. Put the thousand-piece puzzles that your ten-year-old adores higher up, out of direct reach of curious toddlers.

Opposite: Clear plastic bins aren't glamorous, but they keep toys sorted and neat, and they don't draw undue attention (read: look obnoxious) on the shelf. Toys that require supervision (like the cluster of vintage globes) are kept higher and out of reach, but are still accessible when the grown-ups want to include them in playtime.

06

ROTATE
THE TOYS

Toys can easily overwhelm a child. No doubt you've seen a kid surrounded by blinking lights, moving parts, and brightly colored accessories looking entirely bored while announcing that there's *nothing* to play with.

My advice? Don't make all their toys available at once. Leave out some favorites and a few that haven't gotten as much play as you expected, and put the rest in a box or two in a nearby closet. In a few weeks, switch out some of the toys. The Mr. Potato Head parts that were previously so boring will feel brand-new again, full of excitement and possibilities! Just keep switching things every few weeks, and when a new influx of toys arrives with a birthday or holiday, you can rotate them in as you migrate some older ones to the Goodwill donation box.

Above: Baskets of different sizes make it easy to transport toys.
Opposite: Take a look at this room. Can't you imagine a more relaxed and focused playtime when there are fewer toys around?

07

PUT PRETEND PLAY IN THE SPOTLIGHT

My kids love a good costume, and so do I. Ever since our first was a toddler, we've kept a collection of pirate accessories, dresses, ninja bodysuits, tutus, capes, and anything else that could possibly transform a kid into a superhero ready to save the day.

For years we stuffed them in a trunk, until we discovered that they got twice as much use if we hung them at kid eye level. A tidy dress-up outfit on a hanger is far more appealing (and likely to get used) than one crumpled at the bottom of a trunk. And speaking of tidy, I'm quite selective about what stays in our dress-up drawers; once the line of sequins is dragging down the back, it's pitched, unless it can be repaired easily.

There are several ways to hang the dress-up clothes. A kid-size rolling rack is both adorable and functional. You could use a closet rod hung low in a small space. Or install a series of wall hooks within reach of little arms. A small armoire or cabinet with a hanging compartment would also work. Just make it easy for your kids to see what the options are.

Left: I love this DIY ombré dresser, painted with four different shades of pink. Opposite: These unusual wall hooks, shaped like branches, are beautiful even when they're empty. And the dresses on display feel like part of the room's decor.

08

GIVE YOUR PERFORMER A STAGE

If you have entertainers in the house, think about where their performances will happen as you're putting your family room together. Perhaps a low, deep window seat can function as a stage. Or maybe the toy shelves will make a colorful backdrop. If you know you'll be making a thousand videos of your child singing her favorite song of the moment, you might as well know where the best background and lighting is in the family room.

I know a grandfather who is a woodworking hobbyist. He made a tiny "stage" for his grand-daughters' playroom. A portable platform, maybe fourteen inches deep, four feet wide, and no more than three inches off the ground. He knew his granddaughters well. There wasn't a toy in that room that got more play than the "stage."

In our house, we don't have a stage, but we do have a kid-size podium that I found on eBay. It's a lightweight little thing on wheels that we painted fire-engine red. The kids use it to practice reciting poems for their school's Parents' Day. They take turns addressing us from behind it during family meetings. They use it to give pretend speeches. There is something about a stage or podium that gives a bit more gravity to the proceedings, and it's a nice on-ramp to future public performances.

Opposite: Note the world map wall decals by Pop & Lolli. They're made of fabric, and you can reposition them as often as you like.

09

A HAPPY HIDEAWAY

Never underestimate the power of a nook, no matter how tiny: a Harry Potter–esque space under the stairs, a table in a sunny corner of the basement, or a pile of pillows behind the sofa. Carving out a space just for your kids and no one else makes magic—part of being a family that works well together is getting away from each other every once in a while.

I'm reminded of that saying, "If you never leave, how will you know what it feels like to come home?" Taking time away from each other makes coming back together feel like a treat. To a child, hiding away in a private nook is as rejuvenating as a vacation or an inspired day at work. (While we're talking about hiding away, do I need to mention that the same goes for adults in the home? Thirty minutes to yourself and by yourself—even if you can't leave the house—refills your patience tank when you're running on fumes.)

In our house, we have a reading loft in the family room with a soft rug, floor pillows, a comfortable reading chair, a warm throw blanket, and shelves packed with books the kids love. It's set apart, and we parents try to stay out of it. It's a place for the kids to escape to and we want them to feel like it's theirs.

Above: A cushioned window seat with lots of comfy throw pillows like this one is exactly what comes to mind when I think about curling up with a good book. If you don't have a built-in, you can create one with a storage chest topped with pillows.
Opposite: This collapsible tent—a total kids'-fantasy hideaway—stores flat so you can slide it under a bed or keep it at the back of a closet.

10

FOOLPROOF TRICKS FOR STYLING YOUR BOOKSHELVES

When I was growing up, my mom had a full wall of built-ins in the family room, filled with books in every category, and for every age and interest, mixed in with Navajo pottery, framed artwork, a vase of flowers, carved paperweights, a basket, and all sorts of pretty things; part practical, part beautiful. She is really good at keeping shelves looking fresh and interesting. It's an art—but one you can learn.

If your family has a lot of books, try stuffing the shelves. Fill in every available spot from top to bottom. Start by standing books neatly in a row, but then keep adding and adding anywhere you can till the shelves look absolutely overstuffed. Slip sideways books on top of the standing books. Tuck your tiniest volumes into the spare corners. The impression it gives is that your family *loves* books. That you welcome any book that lands on your

doorstep. That you always make room for one more. And the mix of titles and textures is a natural draw. Your children and houseguests will explore the overstuffed shelves until their finger lands on something they hadn't noticed before. Next thing you know, they'll be curled up in your comfiest chair reading a book you forgot you even owned.

Does this approach feel too haphazard to you? Try this instead: Line your books up in any order you like—by format, by topic, or both. Then align all the spines to the front of the shelf. This simple idea will instantly make even the most casual home library feel more formal and official.

Opposite: These bargain shelves are made from backless crates attached directly to the wall to save floor space—with room between to add more and more and more books. This would be an easy project for any DIY-er and would look good wherever you keep books: the bedroom, the family office, the living room, even in the kitchen for cookbooks.

11

DIVIDE AND CONQUER YOUR HOME LIBRARY

We're kind of separatists when it comes to our books! Let me explain. The books we keep in the living room are meant to reflect what's going on in popular culture, current events, and our of-the-moment family interests. Books about crafting and DIY are generally found in the family office. The stories we're reading during this week's bedtimes are waiting on our nightstands. But the family room is all about relaxing, so the books we keep in here are more about leisurely reading: thrillers, our best-loved series, a little chick lit, beach reads, every Caldecott book I've collected, and all the picture books we adore. Some of the books are organized as series, others are arranged by color (a fun strategy for any bookshelf), and the options for the younger ones are always within easy reach.

Above: We built these simple crate-style boxes for the reading loft in our current home. There are three sizes (plus the triangle), and since they're freestanding, they can be reconfigured easily, or even separated and moved to other rooms. If you'd like to make some, you can find instructions at DesignMom.com/book.

12

PLAY THE HOUSE LIBRARIAN

In some families, book collections seem to grow like weeds with every elementary school book fair, birthday, and walk by a bookstore. It certainly happens at my house.

Once a year or so, take an objective look at your library. Does it reflect your family as it is right now? Do you need to add a book about your daughter's new passion, scuba diving? Have you been talking to your kids about racism and need a recommended text to help you find the right words? Is it time to donate some books, and borrow a few others from the library? Put some in storage for future grandkids? Keep your home library up-to-date to ensure that it gets used.

Above: I confess, sometimes I keep books that no one in the family intends to read, simply because they're beautiful!

13

YOUR WALLS SHOULD TELL YOUR FAMILY'S STORY

I think of the family room as more relaxed and more personal than the living room. So if you're lucky enough to have this extra room in your house, why not take the opportunity to show off art or artifacts that tell some of your personal story?

Wall art in the family room is a chance to make your priorities and family values readily apparent. You adore your kids (of course!), you love road trips, and you're obsessed with the young Elvis. With a glance at the walls of your family room, I can see all that about you in an instant, and whatever else you want me to know as well. Create a family room gallery that means something to everyone in the family, and it will keep some of your happiest memories at the ready.

Above: These frames have backs with hinges, so it takes only a second to switch out last week's finger-painting masterpiece for this week's construction-paper collage.

CELEBRATE THE EVERYDAY: 5 MEANINGFUL DISPLAYS

1. CHILDREN'S ARTWORK: A family portrait drawn by your first grader, the series of sun-dye prints they made with Grandma—framed with a wide mat, even the most childlike scribbles will look museum-worthy.

2. FAMILY PHOTOS: Frame family memories to keep them safe and fresh in your family's minds. Photos from your last vacation. Candid shots snapped when you had a family portrait photographed. A series of Polaroids. Any style or any size can work.

3. MEMORABILIA: Why frame only photographs? How about the number that was pinned to your T-shirt during the marathon you ran? A handwritten letter? Postcards from your favorite museum? What about the program from your daughter's first ballet recital, or the ticket stub from your first concert? Framing them tells your family that these personal landmarks, and the things you do together, matter.

4. MAPS: Hang a map of Illinois to show where you studied. Display a map of your hometown—the place your kids have spent a week every summer visiting cousins. You could display a map of Europe, with pins indicating where you've traveled. Or maybe put a map of India on the wall, to show where you *want* to travel. Maybe it's an oversize world map, so your family can see the whole Earth, and consider how they fit into it.

5. QUOTES: Near our reading loft is a framed, handwritten image with two words: "Read instead." It's there to remind the kids that there's a comfy chair and a good book waiting for them when they're done putting together that fort. What quotes are meaningful to your family? Or the better question: What quotes do you wish were meaningful to your family? You get to decide. And whatever words you choose, if they live on the family room wall for a few years, they will remain with your kids for a lifetime.

PREPPING FOR FAMILY PHOTOS

Family portraits are a part of childhood every bit as much as yearly school pictures. They may not happen every year, and there seems to be some amount of stress around them—something about getting everyone to look at the camera at the same time with a not-strange expression on anyone's face. But despite the challenges, they're such a treasure! Your kids will love looking at them as children, and even more as adults. Here's my best advice for family photos.

1. REMEMBER, THEY'RE JUST KIDS!

This is probably the most important thing to keep in mind: Your kids are not paid professionals, and they're going to get worn out during photo shoots pretty fast. A good family photographer will know this and work fast (which is why tips #3 and #4 are so important). As parents, we try to bring an extra measure of patience to the day of a big family photo shoot, and we do our best to keep things upbeat. And if bribes work with your kids, a pack of tiny not-melty candies can work wonders.

2. MINIMIZE COSTS BY USING CLOTHES YOU ALREADY OWN.

Outfitting a whole family can be expensive. After back-to-school shopping (when everyone's wardrobe is looking fresh) is a great time to schedule a photo shoot. If your family loves to ski and there's head-to-toe skiwear in everybody's closets, plan a ski-themed shoot and you won't have to buy a stitch of clothing. And feel free to mix and match between closets to maintain a certain look: a brother wearing his sister's scarf. A daughter wearing her dad's hat.

3. PLAN AHEAD!

Secure any props in advance and scout a location. Again, plan around the resources you have, like the vintage car your father-in-law restored or the swing set at your local park. Is there a pretty view you notice when you're running errands? It might be the perfect backdrop for this year's portrait. Is there a local hiking trail that's meaningful to your family? Sounds like an ideal spot.

4. ARRANGE FOR EXTRA HANDS.

If you're planning a big shoot, with props involved, and you have only a short time with the photographer, bring help! A family friend or a familiar babysitter. Someone to entertain the young ones while the shot gets set up, or who can run a last-minute errand.

5. YOU DON'T HAVE TO MAKE IT ELABORATE.

Putting together a big, coordinated photo shoot takes real time and real work. It's not the sort of thing everyone would enjoy doing. And you can totally go for simple instead—some of our favorite family photos were taken with no planning whatsoever.

14

STORING ARTWORK AND HOMEWORK

The amount of artwork, crafts, school projects, and homework that your child will bring home from preschool through senior year is staggering. Before you start saving all this stuff, think ahead to where it will go, and when and how you plan to access it.

I recommend a folder in your file cabinet for each year of each child's life till they're adults. When they move out, all those files can go into one plastic file box and live in your attic, ready for wedding slide shows or to share with the future grandkids.

In addition to these file folders, I recommend one "treasure box"—a sturdy, shoebox-size lidded container that can hold some of the 3-D objects that neither you nor your child can manage to get rid of. My own treasure box from my childhood includes a sequined glove from a Michael Jackson lip sync performed in front of the high school!

Left: Before you store or say good-bye to your child's artwork, try this clever idea: Pin a long piece of ribbon or yarn along a wall, securing it every 3 feet or so. Then use clothespins to attach your child's favorite pieces. Instant gallery!

DECIDING WHAT TO KEEP

How much of your children's work can you store without being classified as a hoarder? How much can you toss without breaking the heart of your particularly sentimental child? And what should you do with the stuff that you do keep? All good questions! Though the answers might vary if you have five kids instead of one, or if you live in a city apartment rather than a suburban rambler, the same principles apply.

First, you don't need to keep everything. Once your children start their adult lives, ten moving boxes' worth of memorabilia you've collected on their behalf will be just too much stuff to deal with, so be ruthless in your editing. Keep what's meaningful and that which your kids can't bear to part with, and Instagram the rest! Here are a few specific tips.

HOMEWORK: Save the assignments that represent challenges your children overcame, the work that made them proud—essays or writing samples are some of my personal favorites to save. Toss the rest. A handful of representative pieces from an entire year of schoolwork will be plenty. Five pieces of homework multiplied by twelve years of school equals a box full.

2-D ARTWORK: If it's a piece that the entire class made in an identical way, it's really an exercise in motor skills more than in creativity. You don't need to keep it. But if there is a piece that required imagination, and your child loves it, add it to the homework favorites you're saving.

3-D PROJECTS: When it comes to 3-D projects (artwork or science fair or otherwise), if the objects are small, say a gymnastics trophy or a pinewood derby car, first put them on temporary display in your child's bedroom or the family room. When new triumphs come along to take their place, move the very best to a treasure box, and toss the rest. For oversize 3-D projects, temporarily display them, then photograph them for documentation before you say good-bye.

15

ARTFUL WAYS TO DISPLAY YOUR KIDS' ART

Some children produce a ton of artwork. If you have a prolific artist in your household (I have two), trying to figure out what to do with all those drawings and paintings can be a challenge.

Ideally, little artists will use sketchbooks, making it easy to keep everything contained. But if not, try building a sketchbook after the fact. Gather loose drawings made on the same size paper (likely 8½-by-11-inch), and have them hardbound or wirebound into one book that will offer decades of enjoyment as they flip through it and remember that year they spent drawing ninjas.

If putting art into book form doesn't make sense because of its irregular dimensions or large size or dangling streamers, create a way for it to be displayed. String a wire or sturdy twine across a family room wall, hang a box of wooden clothespins nearby, and let your artist choose which works make it to the gallery.

Scanning and minimizing is another smart and sweet option. You can create a wall poster with a grid of dozens of drawings, each miniaturized to just two inches square, with white space between. If your scanner won't accommodate some of the larger projects you'd like to save, take them to your local copy shop.

Lastly, you can also put artwork to work. Use a laminator to make place mats from your son's creations, or turn your daughter's art into your family's postage stamps for the year (you can order them at usps.com). Or simply cover a whole wall with unframed art in lieu of wallpaper. When the wall is full, overlay the old pieces with new ones.

Opposite: This back gallery wall of kid art captures a finger-painting phase. Because the artwork is simply attached with tape, it can be switched out easily as new pieces make their way home.

DOT-PATTERN PORTRAITS
BIG PHOTOS AT A BARGAIN PRICE!

1

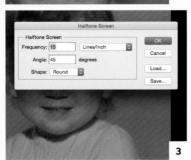

2

3

4

A quick way to bring a whole lot of cool to a room is with an oversize black-and-white photo. But it can be tricky to print a high-quality image at a large size, which is why this project is so genius. This method can make almost any photo—even the tiny snapshot of you in kindergarten—look like it's a big deal. And once you've prepped the photo, you can have it printed at any copy shop that has an oversize black-and-white printer for about $5. This is a super-easy task for anyone who is a photographer or graphic designer, so if it's intimidating to you, ask a buddy for help.

MATERIALS

Photo*

Computer

Scanner (optional)

Photoshop or other photo-editing
    software**

Thumb drive

A high-contrast image works especially well for this technique. If your image is too uniformly gray, use the brightness and contrast tools on your photo-editing software to change it.

**I've written this tutorial for Photoshop, but any photo-editing software will have similar options.*

STEP 1: If your image is a printed photograph, scan it into your computer (or take a digital photo of your photo—the resolution really doesn't matter here). Open the image in Photoshop. Go to IMAGE > MODE > GRAYSCALE. When it prompts you, choose "Discard."

STEP 2: Go to IMAGE > MODE > BITMAP. A Resolution and Method dialog box will appear. For resolutions, type in 300 and choose pixels/inch from the drop-down menu. For method, choose Halftone Screen from the drop-down menu.

STEP 3: A Halftone Screen dialog box will appear. For Frequency, type in 15, and choose lines/inch from the drop-down menu. For Angle, type in 45 degrees. For Shape, choose Round from the drop-down menu. At this point, if the image isn't looking how you want it to, try a different angle, shape, or frequency.

STEP 4: Once you have an image you're happy with, resize it to the scale you want to print. Go to IMAGE > IMAGE SIZE. An Image Size dialog box will appear. For Document Size, type in the dimensions you want your image to print at. Keep the resolution at 300 pixels/inch.

STEP 5: Save the file, then transfer it to a thumb drive. Take the thumb drive to your favorite copy shop and print your poster.

THE LAUNDRY ROOM & THE BATHROOM

Let's talk about bathrooms and laundry rooms. Between the two of them, they carry the heavy responsibility of keeping the whole family shiny and clean. They're unusual spaces because they're used in fits and starts. Most of us don't spend too much time on any given day in the bathroom or laundry room, but when they are in use, we really put them to work.

In the laundry room, there's sorting, stain-removing, soaking, drying, and ironing. In the bathroom, among other things, there's showering, brushing, flossing, blow drying, straight ironing, and nail polishing. Then rush hour ends, and the rooms stand quiet for much of the day.

Bathrooms sometimes get the design attention they deserve, with additions like a gorgeous faucet or some pretty tile, though often they are more utilitarian than utopian. As for laundry rooms, I've had all sorts over the years. But in most cases, they were an afterthought, located in a dark basement or in a corner of the garage. Such a shame! Because the rooms designed to help us be fresh and gorgeous should certainly feel fresh and gorgeous, too. Happily, no matter what your current setup is, there are a few basic principles that can improve any laundry or bathroom situation.

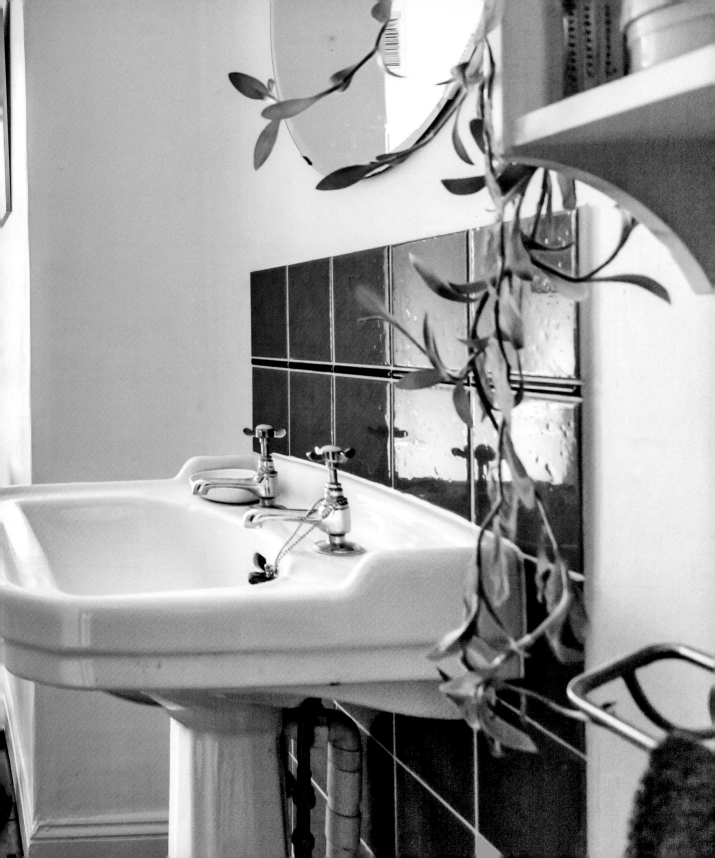

01

PICTURE THE IDEAL, THEN WORK BACKWARD

My ideal laundry room would be the sunniest spot in the house, with lots of windows and natural light. It would have an exterior door for the days when I want to carry a basket outside and line-dry my wash. It would have the most efficient washing machine and dryer on the market. And a deep sink for hand-washing delicate items. There would be shelves for detergent and spot remover and the iron. There would also be low, wide shelves that could hold a couple of laundry baskets. There would be a dock for my phone so I could listen to music while I worked. A hanging rod so I could air-dry items inside when needed. There would be plenty of room to set up an ironing board, plus a place to store it. There would be a generous table or countertop for folding. And there would be a stool for little helpers.

But at the moment, my laundry room isn't a room at all. It's a corner off the kitchen that I have big plans for. Wall it in. Add shelves and wall hooks and a small bench. Maybe switch to a stacking washer and dryer unit to maximize space in the not-very-big corner. Replace the exterior door with a windowed version to let the light stream in. I think it will be super charming.

Your ideal space will probably be different than your current laundry room, too, but that's okay. Picture that pretty room, then work backward, thinking about the realities of the space you're working with. How close can you get to the ideal? Could you shift your washing machine and dryer over by a foot to make extra space? Could you improve the current storage or shelving with wall hooks or organizing bins? Could you add a collapsible drying rack? What about a wardrobe just outside the room to hold an ironing board, pressed laundry, and stacks of extra towels and sheets? There are so many options—many made especially for small spaces. Don't feel like you have to give in to a dungeon-like laundry room.

Opposite: A laundry room with a view? Yes, please. We spend such a big chunk of our lives washing and folding that a sunny little laundry paradise seems as if it would be the first order of business when putting a house together. But alas, a pretty and functional laundry room like this is all too rare.

02

START WITH A CLEAN, WHITE SLATE

Even the dingiest, darkest laundry room or laundry closet can be improved considerably with a scrub-down and a fresh coat of paint. Paint the walls, the ceiling, the door—even the floor if it's a paintable surface—using a bright white or any highly reflective paint color. It is shocking how much this can help make the space feel lighter and more open.

And clean the machines themselves, while you're at it. Take a scrub brush to the linty crevices, or "detail" the machines with a toothbrush. Your washer and dryer might be a decade old, but a little elbow grease will make them much more pleasant to work with, and give you hope that they have plenty of good years left (even if they don't).

Above: In a small space, sticking to one color or a neutral palette makes everything feel less cluttered.

03

YOU NEED TO SEE WHAT YOU'RE DOING

It might seem silly to say that light in a laundry room is important. Duh, right? Yet most laundry rooms I've used over the years—in my home, in relatives' homes, even at roadside hotels—are surprisingly dim or dingy.

So let's restate that light, and lots of it, is key because it makes the room more inviting, of course, but even more important because you need to see what you're doing, especially when dealing with spots and stains. If you have the budget, and it makes sense for the space, feel free to install something gorgeous. But your priority should always be the maximum amount of light, even if the light fixture is nothing to write home about.

Above: A painted ceiling, a painted concrete floor, painted cinder blocks—plus *a ton* of light—and this unfinished basement laundry room is completely transformed.

04

STOCK UP AND STREAMLINE

Doing laundry is a lot like removing a bandage: Do it quickly and the pain will be over before you know it! Preparation is critical; your resolve and interest levels definitely decrease if you don't have the proper tools at your fingertips. So keep everything you need—spot remover, laundry detergent, fabric softener, etc.—close at hand.

If there are sticking points in your routine, you'll find yourself avoiding the task or putting it off. Say you keep your detergent on a shelf above the washer, a natural spot to store it. But you're not the tallest, and the shelf is high, and the bottle/box of detergent is heavy, so every time you need to put in a load of laundry, you have to pull out a step stool, too. It's not the biggest deal in the world, it's just irritating—and one more step in the laundry process. Little annoyances like that add up. So your goal should be to spot the irritations and eliminate as many of them as possible.

Not having your cleaning products stocked up and within easy reach is one of the most common laundry irritations. Think about using space to the side of the machines instead of above them. Or incorporate a rolling cart to hold products if it makes sense for the space. You could also choose products that come in smaller, concentrated forms, or decant your products into smaller containers (see page 225). If your kids are old enough to do laundry, keeping supplies at their level is doubly important, and helps avoid spills.

Opposite: Even your cleaning supplies can be good-looking—and good-looking supplies actually make cleaning more of a joy.

05

MAKE IT PRETTY (I promise, it's worth it)

Once the laundry room is clean, well-lit, and functioning smoothly, you can turn your attention to making it at least a little bit pretty. I know "pretty" often falls on the bottom of the priority list—it can feel like an indulgence, and I get that. But it turns out that if a room is pretty, being in that room is a whole lot more pleasant. A depressing laundry room makes you want to put off throwing in that load of the baby's blankets. But an appealing laundry room will greet you with a smile and draw you in. Particularly if laundry is not your favorite thing to do, making the laundry room as pretty as possible is a smart way to motivate you to tackle the task at hand. A good thing, because in a house with kids, an endless stream of laundry is one of life's constants.

Above: If you approach decorating your laundry room as you would the rest of the house, it won't feel like an afterthought. Consider artwork, plants, a fun mirror—anything that will make the space welcoming.

3 INSTANT LAUNDRY ROOM UPGRADES

1. HANDSOME CONTAINERS FOR DETERGENT:
Get rid of that oversize neon orange box of detergent, and say good-bye to the heavy bottle of fabric softener with the cheesy label—decant your laundry powders, pods, and liquids into prettier containers instead. The new containers don't need to be fancy or expensive; an old widemouthed canning jar is the perfect vessel. It takes only a minute to make the switch, and the pretty bottles on the counter are guaranteed to give your laundry room a lift.

2. A GOOD-LOOKING LAUNDRY BASKET:
Not all laundry baskets are created equal. There are about a million cheap plastic options out there that do the job but beg to be hidden in a cupboard because they are such an eyesore (and don't actually *fit* in a cupboard because they're too big). But do a little research and you'll find some handsome options on the market as well. Whether it's made from wicker, antique-looking wire, or fabric stretched over a metal frame, choose a basket that you can live with when you start folding laundry in the family room and don't finish for three days.

3. A FRESH COVER FOR YOUR IRONING BOARD:
If your ironing board is stored out in the open in your laundry room, it's making a statement—whether you want it to or not. So it might as well make a cheery, positive one! Switch up the cover for something in a broad, preppy stripe or a sunny polka dot. Or opt for a traditional, but modern-looking, metallic silver cover. Then lean the ironing board against the wall, cover facing out, and you'll be happy to see it every time you come in to switch a load.

06

SAVE UP YOUR SPECIAL-ATTENTION LAUNDRY

When we lived in France, ironing was almost a daily task, because it's generally expected that every single item that goes through the laundry will be ironed. Daily attire is a little more formal there, and wrinkled pants or school shirts just won't do. But here in the States, we do far less ironing. I let the ironing basket fill over a week or so, then tackle it in one evening when we're all working together in the kitchen.

The same is true of hand-washing and dry cleaning. I let a basket fill over time. We don't do a ton of hand-washing or dry cleaning, so "over time" can translate to several weeks at our house.

When I can see I have an hour's worth of hand-washing gathered, I'll set aside time to work on it. Again, I like to do tasks like this when the family is already working together anyway—while some of us do dinner dishes, others can tackle the hand-washing.

And dry cleaning? Drop-off and pickup get added to our list of errands as needed. During our New York years, dry cleaning (which included getting Ben Blair's shirts washed and starched) was a weekly errand, but these days, unless it's an investment piece of clothing that I expect to wear for a very long time (like a wool coat or a good suit), I don't take a thing to the dry cleaner.

Opposite: A wire basket is made delicates-safe with the addition of a lining in canvas, the ultimate workhorse material.

07

DON'T PUT ALL YOUR LAUNDRY IN ONE BASKET

To keep your laundry room running efficiently, you'll need more than one laundry basket. In fact, you might need six! You'll need a basket for the hand-washable laundry. You'll need a basket to collect dry-clean-only pieces. You'll need a basket for the mending. If you like to line-dry, you'll need a take-this-outside basket. You'll need a basket to gather a stack of need-to-be-ironed pieces as they come from the dryer. And then, of course, you'll need a basket to carry the clean, folded laundry to the bedrooms.

These don't have to be baskets, actually. For the dry-cleaning, a bag might make more sense. For the collected ironing, a stack on the shelf above the washer might work. A small bin may be all that you need for your mending. Just make sure you have a spot and a plan for all the types of laundry you encounter regularly.

Opposite: I love an industrial laundry bin. Of course it's functional in the laundry room, but it's cute as a hamper in the bedroom as well.

08

STORE THINGS WHERE YOU'LL ACTUALLY USE THEM

There are a number of items other than laundry supplies that are traditionally kept in a laundry room. A sewing kit and a jar of buttons for minor mending. An iron and an ironing board. Perhaps a shoe polish kit. But they don't have to go here. You may find you're more likely to keep up with the ironing if the ironing board and iron are kept in your bedroom closet or close to a television. Putting a mending basket next to the chair with the best natural light makes sense. If you like to keep your shoes by the front door, have a handsome box with shoe polish and brushes there, too, at the ready for a quick scuff

removal. Observe your clothing maintenance habits, take stock of the space available, then store items where they are most likely to get used.

Similarly, if you have all your shoe polish supplies carefully organized on your laundry room shelf but haven't used them in a year because your family pretty much only wears sneakers, then toss those supplies and free up the space. It can be tough to throw or give away "just-in-case" supplies, but an empty shelf always wins over a shelf storing dusty items that aren't being used.

Opposite: Step 1: Move your ironing board to your bedroom. Step 2: Make sure it's so cute you don't want to hide it in the back of the closet.

CUSTOMIZED LAUNDRY BAG

LEARN A TECHNIQUE YOU CAN USE IN A MILLION WAYS

This project is as much an excuse to learn this easy and endlessly adaptable glue-resist technique as it is to make your new favorite laundry bag. Here's the basic idea: Use regular white school glue to create a pattern, words, shapes, or whatever strikes your fancy on a piece of fabric. You can even trace a design or a font with the glue. We're using a king-size pillowcase here, but you could use a cloth napkin, a dish towel, a T-shirt—any cotton fabric is an option. Once the glue is dry, you dye the fabric. Then you wash the fabric out and voilà! The glue washes out, too, and whatever you drew with the glue remains.

MATERIALS

King-size pillowcase or other cotton fabric

Wax paper

Washable liquid glue, like white or gel Elmer's

Carbon paper or paper and a pencil (optional)

Fabric dye

5 to 6 feet of cotton twine or thin rope

Safety pin

STEP 1: Place your desired design underneath the fabric, with wax paper between the pattern and the bottom side of the fabric, and trace the text or pattern with glue. If the fabric is thick and you can't see the design through it, use carbon paper (or paper you have covered in pencil graphite). Put the graphite surface facedown on the pillowcase and place the design on top. Then trace the pattern onto the pillowcase. The transfer may be really faint, and that's fine.

STEP 2: Fill in the outlines with glue then allow the glue to dry completely.

STEP 3: When the glue is dry, follow the manufacturer's directions for the fabric dye and dye the pillowcase. Wash and then dry the pillowcase.

STEP 4: On the cuff of the pillowcase, at the seam, make a ½-inch cut through one layer of fabric. Add a safety pin to the end of your twine, and then push the safety pin through the cuff of the pillowcase until it comes out through the original hole. Remove the safety pin and knot the ends of the twine.

ORGANIZING THE LAUNDRY PROCESS

Keeping up with any chore always comes down to getting a good system in place. Here's how laundry generally works for us.

STEP 1: Hampers are placed in each bedroom (see page 162 for more on my hamper strategy). There's one basket per two people.

STEP 2: When a basket is full, the kids bring it to the laundry room before they head off to school. Sometimes, everyone brings laundry on the same day, but usually it arrives a basket at a time. (Sometimes, this step requires a reminder!)

STEP 3: When the kids leave for school, I make the rounds, straightening the house, doing the breakfast dishes, generally tidying—and part of that is sorting, spot-cleaning, and starting a load of laundry. This is also when I set aside anything that needs special attention like mending or hand-washing. We have two baskets assigned to collect specialized laundry. One basket holds hand-washing and items that should be dry-cleaned. The other basket holds ironing and mending. (What happens to the specialized laundry? See page 226.)

STEP 4: When the kids get home from school (and following an after-school snack), if there's laundry to be folded, we'll work on it together, setting aside anything that needs ironing, while we chat about the day. With two or three of us working, a load of laundry is folded in a few short minutes.

STEP 5: Then comes the trickiest part: actually putting the laundry away. The kids are good about taking their folded laundry to their rooms, but putting it away doesn't often happen without parental encouragement. So at the end of the day, as I'm going from room to room for bedtime routines, I make sure they've returned their clean clothes to drawers and closets. It ends up being a morning-till-night process, but happily, it requires only a few minutes of attention during the day.

SOMETHING TO KEEP IN MIND: As you experiment with your laundry routines to see what works best for your family, know that the system that sounds best in your head might not work in reality. Once upon a time, in an effort to make our laundry routine more efficient, I tried sending the clean laundry back to kids' rooms unfolded, thinking the kids could fold it and put it away right there in the bedroom. But alas, it didn't work. By the time I came in to check the laundry status at the end of the day, the unfolded clean laundry would be mixed with newly dirty laundry, and it would be a confusing mess. If you decide to task your kids with folding their laundry on their own, proceed with caution!

09

THE LAUNDRY ROOM CAN DO MORE THAN LAUNDRY

If you do actually have a dreamy laundry room (hooray!), be sure you're putting it to work. Can it be both a laundry room and an art room? That deep sink would be perfect for washing out paintbrushes. Could you keep your sewing machine on the folding table? You're much more likely to attempt a Halloween costume or hem those double-cuffed pants if the sewing machine is all set up and ready to go.

If your family handles laundry in just two days each week, there is a world of options for what the laundry room can be the other five days! Whatever your situation, see if you can maximize how the room is used. Is there space to hold the recycling bins or an easel? Can your laundry room act as a mudroom, too? What about turning it into an extra storage room, by adding racks and filling them with your luggage and your holiday decorations? Even if it's not the prettiest room in the house, a room that is clean and functional and serves your family daily will be a room that you feel lucky to have.

Above: These solid, adjustable laundry-room shelves are endlessly useable. They're sturdy enough to hold the heaviest boxes but refined enough to host china and stacked linens.

TEACHING KIDS TO DO THEIR OWN LAUNDRY

Technically, kids can learn how to do the laundry the same way they would learn any chore. Once they're old enough to sort the clothes, reach the dials, and measure the detergent, they could probably work laundry into their chore rotation.

I haven't opted for that, simply because doing laundry is my main opportunity to take stock of their clothing. I notice the hole in the knee of a pair of dungarees and can set them aside for patching before it gets worse. I see a grass stain that didn't wash out. I realize it's time for new socks because two pairs have holes. I catch the sequined leotard that is supposed to be dry-cleaned before it goes through the wash and is ruined. Until kids are old enough to care what they look like as they head off into the world, a lot of those details get missed.

But once they actually care about their clothes, kids suddenly have a good reason to know how to do laundry. So when your tween or teen asks if her track uniform will be clean for the meet tomorrow, it's a good opportunity to say, "My plate is too full today, but I'm happy to remind you how to do it if you'd like to throw in a load."

Happily, learning to do laundry is a finite skill set. You don't have to keep learning it over and over again. You'll explain to your kids what the dials on the washer mean, how to measure detergent, how to sort their clothes. They'll make mistakes now and then—washing a red sock with white T-shirts and dyeing them pink, or using bleach to get out a spot and splashing some on their black jeans. But after just a few laundry mishaps, they'll understand how it works and be able to tackle their laundry confidently. So if you're not up for teaching your ten-year-old the laundry how-tos, don't stress. You can always squeeze it in the summer before he leaves for college!

10

THE INGREDIENTS FOR A KID-FRIENDLY BATHROOM

For a bathroom that fosters independence and responsibility, I recommend three things. First, make the sink reachable. Put a sturdy stool in the bathroom that doesn't mind water and has some treads or texture on the surface to keep it slip free. The goal is for your toddler to easily climb onto the stool and then be able to reach the soap and water to wash his hands. If he likes water play, he will also make good use of the stool to fill and empty cups of water over and over and over and over again.

Second, make sure the mirror is low enough for young children to see themselves in it. Even with a stool, in the average American bathroom, the mirror will be too high. That's no good. Trying to learn to brush your teeth without a mirror is futile. Same with learning to brush your hair. So take a peek at the view from their height and then rehang the mirror if necessary, or install an additional one where they can see their reflection with ease.

Lastly, keep a box (or two) of Band-Aids within their reach, in a drawer or cupboard below the counter. When your daughter gets a boo-boo, she'll feel more in control knowing she can access the Band-Aids all by herself. Even better, when your son's friend is over for a playdate and has a tumble, your son will go running for the Band-Aids and get a positive experience with empathy.

Opposite: My favorite approach to designing a bathroom is to begin with a clean white slate and add colorful accents like stools, towels, and bath soaps. Also note the double faucet in this cute, extra-wide sink.

11

MAKE TOWEL ASSIGNMENTS

You might be a family that shares one bathroom in a city apartment. Or you might have a house with several bathrooms and designate one especially for the kids. Either way, to keep towel laundry at a minimum and keep germs to their owners, it's a good policy to assign a bath towel to each member of the family.

We've done this two ways. First, we accented a mostly white bathroom with a full rainbow of towels. Each child had their own color. This meant there were never unpleasant surprises, like grabbing a towel as you climb from the shower and realizing it's still damp from the last person who used it. And the towels added such a fun jolt of color to an otherwise boring bathroom.

The second way we've assigned towels is with ribbon. All the towels were the same color, but we sewed a different color or patterned ribbon loop onto each towel. This is a more subtle way of making the assignments, and makes sense if you're trying to keep a particular color scheme in your bathroom.

Of course, you can also buy your towels from a store like Lands' End or Pottery Barn Kids and take advantage of their custom embroidery. Add names or initials to your towels and say good-bye to any towel confusion.

Opposite: In our house, six kids means we use every color of the rainbow (though June keeps asking for pink!).

12

GET THE TOWELS OFF THE FLOOR

You want your kids to hang up their towels after a bath or shower. And your kid wants to make you happy. But towel bars are not the easiest thing in the world for a kid to navigate. If the towel is thick, folding it neatly and getting the double thickness over the bar is more than you can expect of a little one. And if the bar is high enough to keep the towels off the floor, then it's probably too high for young kids to easily reach.

So take down the towel bar and install easy-to-use wall hooks instead. Hanging becomes a one-step, uncomplicated process. And if you have lots of people sharing the same bathroom, wall hooks also offer the ability to hang more towels in less space.

One last note on wall hooks in the bathroom: If you find the towels are slipping off the hooks, add a little ribbon loop on the long edge of the towel, right in the middle. You can sew it on with a few sturdy stitches or take it to a tailor if your sewing skills are nonexistent. Your kids will place the loop on the hook and you'll have a no-fail way of keeping the towels off the floor and making sure they get a chance to dry out.

Opposite: Nameplates, made out of old-school metal drawer labels, make it easy to remember whose towel is whose.

13

THINK OUTSIDE THE TOILET PAPER DISPENSER

Bathroom floor plans aren't always ideal, and often, the toilet paper is mounted to a wall that's simply not within reach of a seated child's relatively short arms. And if you're working with a spring-loaded toilet paper dispenser, it's easy for you to switch out an empty roll for a full one, but it's not easy at all for a young child. In a house with kids, these little frustrations can add up fast. And so often, they are simply a matter of mechanics.

So if you're dealing with toilet paper issues at your house, bypass them altogether by skipping the toilet paper dispenser. From Lowe's to Ikea to Restoration Hardware, many home-improvement and design stores are now offering unique toilet-paper-storage options, including baskets and vertical stackers. Keeping a stack on hand means toilet paper is always within easy view and easy reach of your kids, and when one roll runs out, the next one is ready and waiting.

Opposite: Decorating your bathroom and not sure where to start? Use a piece of art as inspiration for the entire room. Here, the yellows in the elephant print are highlighted in the shower curtain and bath mat.

14

GROOMING DOESN'T HAVE TO HAPPEN IN THE BATHROOM

If your bathroom is experiencing gridlock on busy school mornings, or at bedtime, the fastest fix is to move some of the grooming tasks to another location. Yes, brushing and flossing teeth is a bathroom-centric task, but brushing hair doesn't need to be.

A small table and a wall mirror in a bedroom can become a simple vanity. Your daughter can do her hair braiding, lip-glossing, and selfie-taking there, freeing up the bathroom for someone who needs a shower. Your son can keep his deodorant and comb in his dresser, so that he's in and out of the bathroom in a flash when it's school prep rush hour.

Which reminds me . . . If you are a family of long-haired folks, keep extra hairbrushes on hand as well. Braiding and hair brushing tend to migrate to the couch when a favorite show is on, or to a bedroom when a sleepover is in the works. To avoid frantic screams of "Where's the brush?!" on crazy mornings, we like to keep a drawer full of hairbrushes.

Opposite: A small desk makes the best vanity. It doesn't take up much space, and it's designed for a chair or stool to fit neatly beneath.

15

THE TWO-MINUTE TIDY

Walking into a bathroom, bleary-eyed and yawning on a tough morning, then stepping over a towel on the floor and up to a counter that is smudged with toothpaste and looking into a sink that hasn't been rinsed out is just gross. Even the biggest slob in the family wants the chance to clean her face in a clean room.

Make a habit of taking two minutes to tidy the bathroom each day (some days, you may need to do so several times). Put the lid on the toothpaste, hang the towels, put the hair clips in the drawer, and wipe down the counter. I'm not talking about a deep clean—that will happen once a week or as often as your family likes to give the bathroom a good scrub. This is just a quick and simple wipe down to make sure the bathroom is ready to greet its next occupant.

Particularly if you have several people using the same bathroom, this small thing makes the sharing much more doable, and keeps the complaints and exasperation at bay. And it's a chore that kids can take responsibility for at a young age, from say about four and up.

Opposite: Healthy plants keep a room looking fresh and clean the air. There are sizes that work on the floor, on shelves, or even hanging from the ceiling. Consider tropical plants for the bathroom—they love the humidity.

THE FAMILY OFFICE

When many of us think of a home office, we picture a small room off the front door with a desk and a computer, maybe some forest-green wallpaper featuring mallard ducks. It's a room mostly used to pay the bills. I remember the kids in *The Brady Bunch* knocking on Dad's home office door when they needed to have a heart-to-heart talk.

But we approach the home office very differently. We think of it as the family office, and we make space for everyone to do their thing.

I try to make it as easy as possible for my kids to escape to the family office and create something. Knowing there's a space in the house stocked with paints, glues, markers, seemingly endless paper, and a generous work surface, the whole family can approach every homework assignment, every work project, every new hobby with a "we can make that happen" attitude. Our creative space keeps boredom at bay and invites inventiveness. It's an important room.

01

DECIDE WHAT YOUR ROOM WANTS TO BE

Before you buy furniture or make plans for the room, decide how you'll be using your family office. At our house, it's a space to paint, draw, and make projects. A space to research homework assignments. A space to run a business (or two or three). It's the space in which we handle all the paperwork that comes with a family of eight. Your family office may be different. A small desk in the kitchen, with the family computer and a file drawer, may fit your needs. Perhaps your family office looks a lot like an artist's studio, or a library. Or maybe it centers on craft projects, with a sewing machine as the center hub.

Is it the room where math homework will happen? (If yes, perhaps you should install a schoolroom pencil sharpener on the wall.) Is it the room you'll use to pay the bills and work out the monthly budget? (If yes, plan on a file cabinet or two.) Is it the room where your kids can make a papier-mâché model of the eye for the science fair? (If yes, having a work sink in the room will make a lot of sense.) Is it a room that needs to have two desks—one for Mom and one for Dad? (If yes, you may need to get creative about the space.) Once you know what needs to happen in this room, it will be a whole lot easier tackling the hows and wheres.

Opposite: A giant bulletin board transforms an unused wall into a source of inspiration! And because the board and wall are the same color, the focus remains on the artwork.

02

YOU NEED EASY-TO-CLEAN FLOORS THAT DON'T MIND PAINT SPLATTERS

This is one of the spaces in your house where flooring choices matter most. If your project room isn't easily swept or wiped down, it's going to give you a headache. Daily.

Concrete floors really appeal to me, whether they're highly polished or a nice industrial-looking matte version. And although I've been warned that concrete floors can feel cold or unwelcoming, in an office or studio setting they make a lot of sense because they're easy to maintain and can take a beating. But concrete isn't for everyone, whether it's due to budget (concrete can be even more expensive than hardwood!) or its weight, which is sometimes too great for a home to structurally bear.

I also heartily recommend industrial-grade VCT (vinyl composite tile). I've been a VCT advocate ever since we had some installed in the kitchen of our first home, with wonderful results. It's made to withstand high traffic and heavy use (you see it in schools and hospitals), which makes it perfect for an active family. The maintenance is wonderfully easy; you can give it a high shine with polish or keep it matte. Plus, there are dozens and dozens of color options available, so the sky's the limit on creating patterns or a custom design. But one of my favorite parts about composite tile is how well it deals with wear and tear—since the flooring pigment goes all the way through the material, gouges won't show up as off-color scratches. And if you do happen to damage a section of the floor, the fix is a simple replacement of one or two tiles.

Opposite: The concrete floors aren't the only brilliant move in this office: The awkward space under the stairs has been transformed with a laptop-ready desk, a task lamp, inspiring artwork, and a file cabinet—everything you need to handle household paperwork or get your studying on.

03

A WORKTABLE AS BIG AS YOUR FAMILY'S IMAGINATION

Once we had room in our house for a dedicated family office, my first move was to add the biggest work surface I could fit in the space. Having a worktable has made it much more likely that we'll start and finish projects—we can jump in and out of them whenever we have a moment, instead of watching them get stalled out when we clear the table to set it for dinner. In an ideal world, every family would have a project table that isn't asked to perform any duties other than holding their inspiration.

When choosing a worktable, think first about size and durability. Will it fit in the space? Is it big enough that you can unroll wrapping paper or spread out poster board? Can it be scrubbed down? Will drops of dye or bleach harm it? Will scratches ruin it—or will they add to its patina?

You want a table that is good-looking, but it certainly doesn't have to be precious. Go for maximum usability. Picture something that looks like it was salvaged from an office building or a machine shop. It will have to withstand hot glue, acrylics, ink splats, and the weight of geometry books, and double as a fort every so often. Choose something sturdy, perhaps very old and well used—if the table made it through a century of farm life, then surely it can handle a couple of decades with your kids.

Opposite: We built this oversize project table two houses ago. It's right between standard table height and counter height, and it's sturdy (read: heavy) as all get out. And the materials were under a hundred dollars. If you'd like to build one, too, see the full tutorial at DesignMom.com/book.

04

KEEP A DESK AVAILABLE TO ANYONE

I love the idea of a properly appointed personal desk with nooks and crannies that hold treasures, favorite pens, a roll of stamps, and a few ancient love notes. But when many people need to share one desk, as they do in my house, an empty space is more inviting—a clean slate for whoever sits down.

Think about which items will be generally useful to the whole family, and keep them on the desktop: In addition to the family computer, a jar of pencils or pens and a stack of paper in a tray are safe bets. Perhaps a stapler, too, or any other essentials you know all your family members use frequently. Keep any other desk accessories and office supplies in a separate place, like a desk drawer or a nearby cupboard.

Above: Always, always, always take advantage of a window when you can.

05

. . . AND SEATING THAT FITS EVERYONE

Your needs will depend on your worktable and desk, but I've found that adjustable stools are the best office seating option for our family. They take up less space than a full-size office chair and can be easily adjusted to allow for Ralph's long legs and June's little ones.

If you have plenty of space for a traditional desk chair, the same idea works. Choose one that includes a lever for height adjustment. You can lower it when you're checking e-mails, or raise it when your daughter is looking up a YouTube tutorial.

Since there's typically a lot going on in this room, I also prefer stools that allow you to spin around and face another direction while you're seated. That way, when little brother asks big sister for an opinion on the album cover he's creating, she can momentarily turn away from her beading loom to look at the monitor and weigh in.

Lastly, if your house is a hot spot for group school projects, a stack of extra stools or spare chairs will certainly be put to good use—and they can be easily transferred to the dinner table if the group project turns into pasta night.

Above: We found these stools at Crate & Barrel. We started with four and immediately went back for more—we've used them as nightstands, as side tables, and, of course, as seating.

06

MAKE IT A FAMILY COMPUTER

We have a bunch of personal iThings, and Ben Blair and I have our own laptops, but the kids don't. Instead, we have one desktop family computer that lives in the home office, and it's like the brain of the room, helping with homework, playing music, or providing step-by-step instructions for a new project we're tackling. It has a large screen, helpful for editing photos and movies and creating logos, illustrations, and book-report covers.

One other note: As you consider your family computer and where to place it, think about screen privacy and collaboration. If the monitor faces into the room for everyone to see, it's easy to observe the websites your kids are exploring. And if you pull the computer out of the corner, there might be space for several people to crowd around it and collaborate on that T-shirt design for the school choir.

Above: Thank goodness for washi tape. For ever-changing inspiration boards, or temporarily hanging something until you can make a framing decision, nothing is better. It looks good, it comes in a thousand varieties, and the tackiness is light, so it typically won't damage the surface beneath. It's like pretty painter's tape.

07

DID YOU KNOW YOUR PRINTER CAN MAKE MAGIC?

We have one family printer, and it lives near the computer. Most of the time, it functions as a basic workhorse, but sometimes—almost always at the last minute—we need the printer to help us make some magic. We use printable iron-on paper to create custom T-shirts and sheets of Shrinky Dinks to make homemade jewelry. Whether it's eleventh-hour class valentines, spur-of-the-moment birthday party invitations, or science fair display notes, we like the printer to be ready for our whims, so we keep on hand glossy photo paper, card stock in a variety of colors, sticker paper for labels, and a few specialty papers.

Above: Note the way a strong black wall camouflages the printer.

08

LIGHTING THAT'S UP TO THE TASK

Late in the day, our project table turns into a homework zone for the older kids. Crayons are replaced by mechanical pencils as the table gets covered in index cards filled out with world history notes. During the day, the windows offer most of the light we need in our home office, but in the evening, task and overhead lighting become essential.

Our ideal office lighting is overhead lights that are bright enough for the teens to tackle a late-night project with their study group, smaller task lights that allow for more quiet, concentrated study in an otherwise dim room, and small spotlights that bring attention to the prettiest things on the wall.

In my high school wood shop, a pull-down outlet hung over each table. Students could use it to plug in their hand sanders, while leaving the table completely open to hold big projects. This idea is officially on my family office wish list. I'd love a hanging outlet or two over our worktable, so that we can plug in task lights (or glue guns!) without having cords running to the wall and tripping people up.

Opposite: Create your own overhead lighting by taking a task lamp off the table and installing it on a shelf or a wall above.

09

FACE INSPIRATION

Think beyond the computer monitor and determine where you want your gaze to fall when you're searching the air to find a synonym for *wanderlust* (*peregrination* is a good one). If the outdoor view is pretty, placing your desk and computer screen by a window makes sense. But even if you're stuck facing a wall, you can make it a pleasure to behold.

I love an inspiration board above a desk. Staring at an assortment of images and ideas that have inspired me lately can help crack a momentary writer's block, or spark a new DIY idea. It might be a metal sheet with magnets, a cork board with pushpins, or a ribbon board where you can tuck in the pretty bits and pieces you've collected. Fill it with whatever makes you smile or gets your imagination going: a handsome thank-you card, a postcard featuring your favorite work of art, an inspiring quote, a swatch of fabric that matches the colors of the redesign you've been working on for your website. Or your favorite family photos!

Opposite: An inspiration wall that the computer blends right in to, as if it's simply one more source of pretty pictures—delightful! To replicate the anything-goes feeling of this ever-changing wall, hang tear sheets from magazines, postcards, stationery, photographs, drawings, and text.

10

WRANGLE THE OFFICE SUPPLIES

At some point, usually in middle school, your kids' craft stuff begins to overlap with their homework supplies. Slowly but surely, mechanical pencils, pens, index cards, rulers, and pink erasers merge with pom-poms and clay. Figuring out where to put everything is a big challenge.

When I'm plotting out supply storage for a family office, first I consider accessibility. Everything should be easy to find for the kids who need it, but things like X-Acto knives and Sharpies should be inaccessible to little ones. Items that are used most often should be right at hand, while lesser-used items could be stored in a closet.

The solution in our current family office is rolling stacked metal bins. One is filled with jars of crayons and markers and glue sticks, and the other has items like staplers, pencils, index cards, and graphing calculators. The bins move through the room—around the project table or to the desk—as needed. That way they're always close by, without taking up valuable desktop space or cluttering the project table.

Opposite: We have two of these rolling carts in our family office. All our supplies are out in the open, allowing me to see what we need and add it to my shopping list accordingly.

11

FILE IT UNDER "ORGANIZED"

Be realistic about the space you need for paperwork. Are you super organized and keep a file box for each year of your life? Then allot closet space in your office to store those tidy boxes. If closet space is at a premium, just store the most recent two or three boxes in the closet, and put the older ones in a less convenient closet or attic space.

Do you file every piece of paper that comes into your house? Or maybe your office doesn't have a closet? Then go for four-drawer file cabinets, and keep them out in the open. If they're hard to get to, the filing is more likely to pile up and overwhelm the room.

As we enter the digital age and need to keep fewer hard copies, most files can live in the computer and hard copies of important documents can be stored in one place. So you might be better off with just a couple of trays that hold bills to pay and other actionable paperwork.

Managing paperwork is always a challenge at our house, but this is the system that works for us.

First, we shred or recycle as much as possible. If we don't absolutely need to store it, we don't.

Second, we have an "active" accordion file folder in the most convenient drawer in our file cabinet that holds the most often requested documents—copies of birth certificates and immunizations and proof of insurance. When we're registering the kids for school or heading to a doctor's appointment, we can just grab this folder and run.

Next to the accordion folder, we keep the rest of the active paperwork—things like receipts and current tax documents—in bigger folders with more overarching categories. A file for each child. A file for the mortgage. A file for appliance manuals.

Finally, important original documents—marriage certificate, birth certificates, passports, certain financial documents—are kept in a small fireproof box.

It's a good system for our family, and my favorite part is that it doesn't require too much time, and we can find what we need when we need it (mostly!).

Opposite: This low row of filing cabinets is perfectly positioned. When you've completed paperwork at the desk, you can turn around and file anything that needs to be saved, leaving nothing to move, stack, or forget about.

12

A FAMILY CALENDAR KEEPS EVERYONE (and everything) ON THE SAME PAGE

A family calendar is key to making sure everybody is in tune with the family schedule. I keep detailed color-coded calendars on my laptop, but when discussing calendar items with the kids—say, the dates we'll be traveling for Christmas or how someone's swim class schedule will overlap with his guitar lessons—I find an oversize paper calendar to be essential. I've found that it's difficult for young children to pay attention to a computer calendar or a tiny one on a phone. A paper one, with big squares ready for notes, does a better job of reminding kids about upcoming events. And it's also better for building anticipation—seeing paper squares filled in or x-ed out as a birthday approaches is a highlight of each day for a grade-schooler.

The family office is one natural place to keep a family calendar, but you may find you want to discuss the calendar over dinner at the kitchen table, or during a family meeting in the living room. If this is the case, a calendar that comes off the wall easily, and can be moved from room to room, might make the most sense. Whatever type you choose, just make sure it's displayed where the whole family can see it.

Opposite: This magnetized whiteboard calendar is dreamy. The numbered circles move as needed, and you can wipe the whole thing down to start over.

STICKY-NOTE CALENDAR

QUICK, FLEXIBLE, AND THERE WHENEVER YOU NEED IT

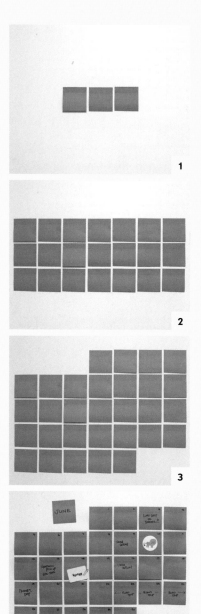

This is so easy it's barely a DIY project. In one sentence: Use square sticky notes to make an instant calendar. I've made them on bulletin boards (no pins needed), directly on the wall, even on windows by the dinner table. And if I need it to be portable, I'll make one on a whiteboard.

When you're planning out your summer, you can see all three months simultaneously, unlike when using a flip calendar. Because the materials are simply sticky notes, it's easy to have them on hand for calendar-making at a moment's notice. You can color-code the days with different colors of sticky notes. And if you make a mistake, or change the schedule, you simply replace the "day" with a new sticky note. Lastly, when counting down dates, kids love removing a square each day, similar to opening doors on an advent calendar.

MATERIALS

Sticky notes

Marker

STEP 1: Decide where you want the calendar to be and place the first square. You're going to work from the middle outward, so the first square you place will be Wednesday of the middle week of the month. Add Tuesday and Thursday of the same week. Step back to eyeball the squares to see if they seem straight.

STEP 2: Finish that middle week with seven squares, then add a row above it and below it to create three full weeks. If the first row was pretty straight, and you follow it as you add more weeks, the whole calendar will turn out pretty straight. And don't worry if it's not perfect. The squares are repositionable if you want to adjust them.

STEP 3: For the top row and the bottom row, you'll add only enough squares to complete the month. How many squares on each row will depend on the month you are creating. I like to double-check on my phone calendar to make sure I'm starting and ending the month on the correct days of the week.

STEP 4: Add numbers with a marker. You can make the numbers big and graphic so they're easier to see at a glance, or if you need writing space, like I do, you can keep the numbers small and put them in the corner. If you like, add one or two more squares at the top so you can write the name of the month.

JUNE

				1	2	3	4
5	6	7	8	9 SWIM LESSON	10	11
12	13 GOODWILL PICK UP 678-5102	14	15	16 SWIM LESSON	17	18
19 FATHER'S DAY	20	21	22	23 ← ROAD TRIP	24 ← ROAD → TRIP	25 ← ROAD → TRIP
26	27	28 POTLUCK BBQ	29	30		

13

CREATE A WELL-STOCKED ART SUPPLY CUPBOARD

Having art supplies at the ready makes it a thousand times easier to get creative with your kids. But if you've never set up an art supply cupboard before, it can be intimidating. Craft stores and art supply stores are huge! The options are overwhelming.

Don't feel like you have to buy one of everything. Start with reliable basics that have proven themselves with millions of kids and millions of families, and then expand from there. If your son loves working with his hands, you could introduce origami. If your daughter takes quickly to a paintbrush, consider letting her experiment with oil colors.

But when you're just starting out, keeping your cupboard stocked with the basics means you'll be ready for pretty much anything your budding artist comes up with.

Above: Fresh art and craft supplies are so pretty! You'll want to store them out of their boxes so you can see all the colors.

NOT SURE WHERE TO START?
15 BASICS TO KEEP ON HAND

1. CRAYONS: My kids like Craypas—they blend well and make really intense colors.

2. COLORED PENCILS: For when crayons just can't give the kind of detail your little artist is imagining.

3. WASHABLE MARKERS: They produce more intense color than crayons and fill in large areas quickly.

4. COLORING BOOKS: There are so many options out there! I personally favor Japanese doodle books, and Hervé Tullet's scribble books.

5. A BIG ROLL OF PAPER: Big paper = big ideas. Look for oversize sheets or a wide roll.

6. WATERCOLOR PAINTS: Some kids really love the interactive nature of watercolors. For the best results, always use the heaviest paper you have on hand.

7. CONSTRUCTION PAPER: The big sheets of solid colors spark ideas, are easy to cut, and are affordable, making them a good option for experimenting.

8. SAFETY SCISSORS: Stock extras!

9. MODELING CLAY: Buy some Play-Doh, buy a naturally made version like those offered by EcoKids, or make your own at home.

10. CRAFT STICKS: You never know what kids will come up with when they have a pile of wooden craft sticks in front of them.

11. PIPE CLEANERS: They're fun to fiddle with and come in handy at unexpected times—like when glue won't work to connect something.

12. GOOGLY EYES: You will be shocked by how many uses your kids will find for these.

13. GLITTER: Glitter makes any project seem special—use it to tempt your kids to the art table.

14. GLUE STICKS: Use the purple kind with little kids so they can see where they've applied glue.

15. LIQUID GLUE: When a glue stick isn't cutting it, this should be your go-to.

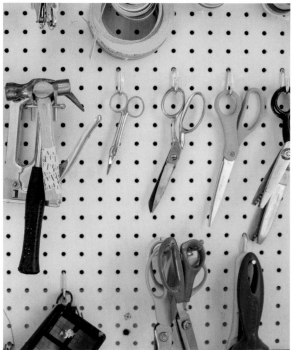

14

KEEP AHEAD OF THE CRAFTING CHAOS

With spare school supplies and party favors and random art projects for playgroup, a ridiculous amount of craft materials come into a family home. The key to keeping them accessible and organized is dealing with the leftovers.

I'm tempted to keep everything. I see those small scraps of paper and know they could be turned into confetti. I see the broken crayons and know we could melt them down for an art project. But if I leave them mixed in with the newer, fresher art supplies, the craft closet (or in our case, craft bins) will look messy and unappealing. And my kids will steer clear of the chaos. If, on the other hand, I'm ruthless about clearing out the old, unused stuff so that the fresh, useable supplies are easy to see and access, my kids approach our craft supplies with delight. In a child's eye, well-stocked, well-organized craft closets are equivalent to a three-ring circus, free pony rides, and snow cones in every flavor—pure magic, joy, and possibility.

Opposite, clockwise from top left: Craft supplies can be stored on an unused wall in a closet; buy a pegboard system on which to hang tools and materials, or freestyle it with an assortment of peg-friendly hooks and handled jars; repurposed kitchen jars do a fantastic job of corralling thread, ribbons, or anything else that's good-looking enough to not want to hide away; a glass-front cabinet lets colorful craft supplies show through.

HAPPILY CRAFTING WITH KIDS: 8 RULES TO REMEMBER

1. IT'S GOING TO GET MESSY. If that stresses you out, cover surfaces with newsprint, butcher paper, or a plastic tablecloth. Use only washable materials. Then try to relax. If you get paint on your hands, it's okay. If your child gets marker on her shirt, it will wash out. When you're finished, roll everything up and discard the mess.

2. IT'S THE IDEA THAT COUNTS. Try not to give your child one firm example of how a craft should turn out. Either don't present an example at all, or present several options, so your child knows he can use his imagination. If he glues the eyes where the ears should be, good for him—think of it as an opportunity to introduce him to Cubism.

3. CRAFTS SHOULD BE AGE-APPROPRIATE AND PLAY TO YOUR CHILD'S STRENGTHS. If the craft is complicated, break it into steps and figure out which ones your child can do. For example, we once made wands for a Harry Potter celebration. My six-year-old chose the paper, but I rolled it up, which required more dexterity than her little hands could muster. She taped the rolled wand up, and I did the hot gluing. She painted the wand with craft paint, and I added metallic highlights with permanent marker.

4. NO HELICOPTER CRAFTING. If you really enjoy crafting yourself, set aside a portion of the craft that is just for you to make. When I don't do this, I hover and am tempted to control what my kids are making. If I reserve some of the craft materials ahead of time, it's easier for me to allow the kids to do their thing.

5. PLAN YOUR CRAFT TO BE DONE IN AN ALLOTTED TIME (IF YOU DON'T HAVE A DEDICATED CRAFT SPACE). If you're crafting on the kitchen table and the craft isn't finished before dinner, it can be frustrating to have to clean it all up and start again later.

6. YOU DON'T HAVE TO KEEP IT FOREVER. Crafts quickly accumulate and take up lots of space (and not everything your child makes is a masterpiece). Say good-bye to some old crafts when new art projects come into your life—before you start resenting crafts in general! Much of the value of crafts is in the making.

7. USE MATERIALS YOU HAVE AT HOME. For everyday crafting sessions, it's not worth running to the store to get the perfect paper or trim or finishing detail. The enthusiasm for the project will evaporate if you have to break for errands.

8. NOT EVERY CHILD LIKES GLUE AND GLITTER AND CUTTING PAPER. Don't force it.

15

KEEP A GIFT CLOSET

Left: This isn't a random hodgepodge of goodies that take up loads of space, but a few choice purchases that make my life easier on a moment's notice.

Since we store our wrapping supplies in the family office, I've found it comes in handy to keep a small stockpile of gifts there as well. Whether I'm in a home accessories shop, a department store, the grocery store, or a boutique, I scour the sale shelves for items that make me smile. I'm not a hoarder, I promise! But I do believe in keeping a well-stocked gift closet (or in our case, gift drawer) for all those happy occasions that pop up in the middle of a hectic schedule.

Currently, I'm storing two blueberry-scented candles scored in a buy-one-get-one deal, a jar of gourmet lemon curd, an adorable stationery kit for kids plus one luxe set that smells like lavender, permanent markers in every color with matching modeling clay, a tiny turquoise vase that I am tempted to fill with baby's breath every time I see it, a cowbell that looks like it's from a faraway land (even though it's not), three of my favorite picture books, and organic hand lotion. I am set for any neighborhood tea, kid's birthday celebration, rainy-day meltdown, teacher gift, or a random "just because I was thinking about you" impulse.

16

AN EASY-TO-PULL-OFF WRAPPING STATION

With eight family birthdays, plus friends' birthdays, Mother's Day, Father's Day, and the December holidays, a lot of gift wrapping happens at our house over a year. So an essential part of our family office is a wrapping station. The term is fancier than the reality: a charming bucket filled with rolls of pretty paper, combined with a drawer of ribbons in every shade, and another drawer of tissue papers, empty gift boxes, and cutout gift tags. That's all you need.

Spread out your wrapping supplies on the empty worktable and turn on some music, and late-night Christmas Eve wrapping becomes a pleasure!

Above: This stainless steel kitchen island feels right at home in a family office. The big wide surface is ideal for rolling out wrapping paper. (And take a look at that handsome fabric-covered bulletin board—learn how to make one on page 170.)

AFTERWORD

I wonder where you are as you're reading this, and whether you're feeling rejuvenated and inspired. I hope you can't wait to implement something or other you've learned from these pages! Oh. What's that? You're feeling overwhelmed? Oh dear. Please don't be overwhelmed. Please don't think you've got to cross everything off your to-do list by tomorrow. There's no deadline. You've got a whole lifetime to work on it.

You've read this book, so I already know you care about creating a wonderful space where your family can thrive. And making a beautiful, happy home is not about what we don't have or what we want to buy. It's all about what we *do* have, and how incredibly priceless it all is. It's about how we spend the days we're given with this family of ours, and making the home we share a place our kids will love to describe to our grandchildren. It's about making our kids' memories delightful.

We can do this. I promise. Because if there's one thing I've learned, it's that there are countless ways to live stylishly and wonderfully with kids. I hope this book helps you find *your* way.

ACKNOWLEDGMENTS

Oh my goodness. I can't believe how many people it takes to make a book! This has been a huge team effort, and there are so many wonderful people I want to thank.

First off, I offer all my love plus a heartfelt thank-you to Ben Blair, who gets credit for all the best parts of my life. To Ralph, Maude, Olive, Oscar, Betty, and Flora June, I offer the best sort of hug and a thousand thank-yous as well. No matter what our home looks like, it never feels quite right when they're not around. They make it really fun to be a parent.

Extra-special thanks with a cherry on top goes to Karey Mackin, who worked with me from the moment this book was conceived—wordsmith-ing, brainstorming, staying enthusiastic when I was discouraged about the startovers—and took on the role of photo organizer and general manager as deadlines loomed. I absolutely could not have finished (or even started!) this book without her.

Of course, it would be impossible to thank my team at Artisan enough. There's Lia Ronnen, who started talking to me about this project in 2010, and who never wavered in her belief that it would be an amazing book, all while gracefully managing the transition from editor to publisher mid-project. Thanks to Bridget Heiking, who didn't panic when I pushed back every possible deadline, and made a calming list for me whenever I was overwhelmed. Thanks to Michelle Ishay-Cohen for the gorgeous layout and art direction, and for being patient with my strong opinions about fonts. Specials thanks also go out to Naomi Mizusaki, Renata Di Biase, Sibylle Kazeroid, and Nancy Murray.

Next, I want to thank my insanely talented sister Jordan, who was a sounding board for me on this project, and opened her home for multiple photo shoots as well. What are the chances I'd have family members who also make their livings as bloggers and that I can talk shop with whenever I need to. I'm a lucky duck.

Thank you to my dear friends Laura Mayes and Laurie Smithwick for being the first people I want to call whenever I get a new business or project idea. My online life and career is forever linked with both of theirs.

Thank you to my longtime contributors, Amy Christie and Lindsey Johnson, for helping me with the DIY projects in this book and accepting my inability to reply to e-mails in a timely manner. Thanks to Kristen Loken, who jump-started my photography block, and to Sarah Hebenstreit for the iconic cover shot.

And finally, the photos in these pages were captured in dozens of beautiful homes around the world. Prepping your home for a photo shoot is no simple task—it's a big commitment of time and patience. So special thanks to the following homeowners for graciously opening their doors, and, in some cases, acting as photographers and stylists as well: Courtney Adamo, Mariana Anderson, Meta Coleman, Sara Davis, Leigh Deighton, Ruth de Vos, Jamie Diersing, Katy Dill, Paul and Jordan Ferney, Tina Fussell, Alexis Garrett, Kirsty Gungor, Laura Hall, Mary Heffernan, Agnes Hsu, Amy Jacobs, Rae Ann Kelly, Jenny Komenda, Kate and Ed Lewis, Erin Loechner, Janette Maclean, Jeanne McGuire, Trina McNeilly, Shannon Molenaar, Jo-Anne Pabst and Grant Taylor, Rachel Peters, Jane Rhodes, Sarah Sandidge, Rachel Shingleton, Liz Stanley, Candice Stringham, Joslyn Taylor, Michelle Turchini, Esther van der Paal, Fleur van Kesteren, and Liz Bell Young.

PHOTOGRAPHY CREDITS

Courtney Adamo: pages 113, 155 (bottom left), 188–89, 193, and 260

Mariana Anderson: pages 148–49

Gabrielle Stanley Blair: pages 15, 202, and 212

Blue Lily Photography (with stylist Gabrielle Stanley Blair): page 207

Nicole Breanne (with stylist Shannon Molenaar): pages 125 (top left), 169, 235, 236–37, and 256

Carpenter Photo (with stylist Sara Davis): page 18 (bottom right)

Amy Christie: pages 104–5 (with calligraphy by Melissa Esplin), 184–85, and 232–33

Caroline Coehorst (with stylist Mirjam Knots): pages 63, 117, 126, 151, 155 (bottom right), 166–67, 178, and 201

Caroline Cohenour (with stylist Emily Hart): pages 132 and 271

Meta Coleman: pages 114, 145, 155 (top left), 156 (bottom right), 192, 198, and 239

Lesley Colvin (with stylist Courtney Adamo): pages 20, 60–61, 156 (top right), 195, and 219

Leigh Deighton: page 127

Katy Dill: pages 252–53 and 278 (bottom left)

Paul Ferney (with stylist Jordan Ferney): page 17

Tina Fussell: pages 51, 128, 262, and 264

Kirsty Gungor: pages 74–75, 102, 108, 152, and 194

Janae Hardy (with stylist Sarah Sandidge): pages 70, 122, and 155 (top right)

Sarah Hebenstreit: (with stylist Rosy Fridman) pages 48–49, 52, 62, 92; (with stylist Gabrielle Stanley Blair) pages 73, 83, 85 (bottom left), 91, 119, 146, and 204

Eliza J. Photography (with stylist Alexis Garrett): pages 82, 88–89, 109, 111, 112, 125 (bottom right), 203, 228, and 278 (top right and bottom right)

Stacy Jacobsen (with stylist Rae Ann Kelly): pages 43 and 156 (top left)

Lindsey Johnson (with stylist Gabrielle Stanley Blair): pages 38–39, 78, 170–71, 274–76, and 281

Micah Kandros (with stylist Amy Jacobs): page 244

Alicia Kealey (with stylist Mary Heffernan): page 130

Becky Kimball (with stylist Jane Rhodes): page 186

Jenny Komenda: page 224

The Land of Nod: pages 55 and 135

Markus Linderoth 160

Kristen Loken (with stylist Gabrielle Stanley Blair): pages 18 (top right and bottom left), 28, 30, 34, 36–37, 65–67, 79, 80 (all), 85 (top left), 96–97, 107, 141, 153, 172–73, 196, 199, 213, 220, 222, 227, 231, 243, 247, 259, 261, 268, and 282, 285

Jeanne McGuire: page 221

Anna Naphtali: pages 24, 44, 68, 85 (top right), 95, 98–100, 164, 176–77, 179–81, 208, 267, and 278 (top left)

Chris Plavidal (with stylist Joslyn Taylor): page 85 (bottom right) and 165

Peggy Saas (with stylist Bec Tougas): pages 18 (top left), 40, 58, 150, 255

Rachel Shingleton: page 27

Kathrin Simon (with stylist Janette Maclean): page 21, 31, 76, and 156 (bottom left)

Liz Stanley: page 162

Candice Stringham: pages 120–21, 138–39, 183, 240, 263, 272, and 283

Grant Taylor (with stylist Jo-Anne Pabst): pages 12–13, 22–23, 71, 106, 125 (top right), 158, 210, and 248

Iris Thorsteinsdottir for Kid and Coe: pages 216–17

Aaron Tokarz (with stylists Kirsten Grove and Trina McNeilly): page 182

Esther van der Paal: 125 (bottom left)

Heather Zweig (with stylist Jordan Ferney): pages 56, 142, and 191